T0382153

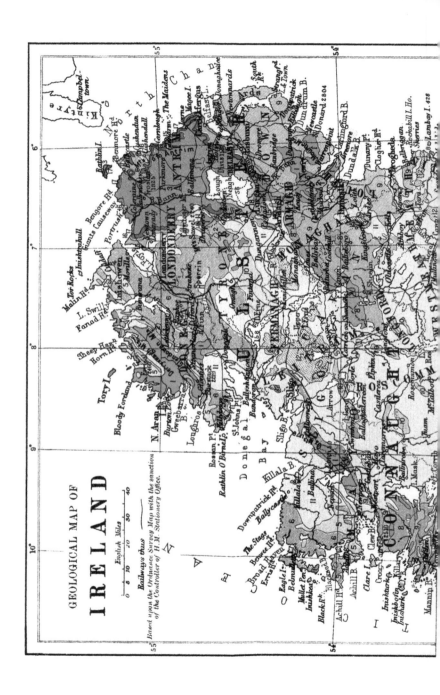

GEOLOGICAL MAP OF
IRELAND

English Miles
0 5 10 20 30 40

Railways thus ——

Based upon the Ordnance Survey Map with the sanction
of the Controller of H.M. Stationery Office.

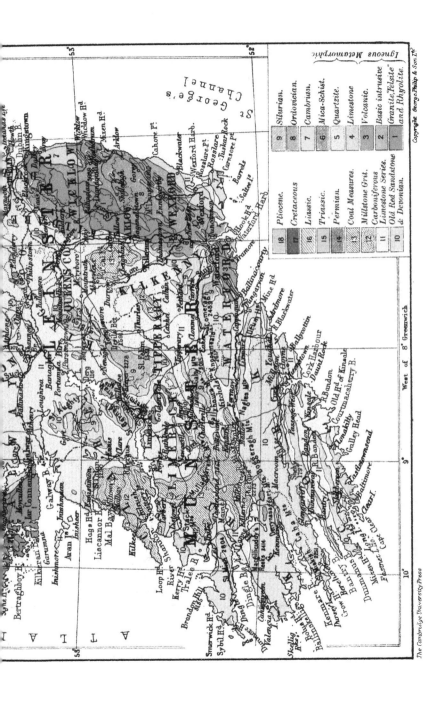

St George's Channel

9	Silurian.	
8	Ordovician.	
7	Cambrian.	
6	Mica-Schist.	
5	Quartzite.	
4	Limestone	
3	Volcanic.	
2	Basic intrusive	Igneous & Metamorphic
1	Granite, "Felsite" and Rhyolite.	

18	Pliocene.	
17	Cretaceous	
16	Liassic.	
15	Triassic.	
14	Permian.	
13	Coal Measures.	
12	Millstone Grit.	
11	Carboniferous Limestone Series.	
10	Old Red Sandstone & Devonian.	

West of 8° Greenwich

Copyright. George Philip & Son.L?ᵈ

The Cambridge University Press

THE PROVINCES OF IRELAND

Edited by

GEORGE FLETCHER, F.G.S., M.R.I.A.

ULSTER

ULSTER

Edited by

GEORGE FLETCHER, F.G.S., M.R.I.A.

With Maps, Diagrams and Illustrations

CAMBRIDGE
AT THE UNIVERSITY PRESS
1921

CAMBRIDGE
UNIVERSITY PRESS

University Printing House, Cambridge CB2 8BS, United Kingdom

Cambridge University Press is part of the University of Cambridge.

It furthers the University's mission by disseminating knowledge in the pursuit of education, learning and research at the highest international levels of excellence.

www.cambridge.org
Information on this title: www.cambridge.org/9781107511422

© Cambridge University Press 1921

First published 1921
First paperback edition 2015

A catalogue record for this publication is available from the British Library

ISBN 978-1-107-51142-2 Paperback

EDITOR'S NOTE

THE aim of this series is to offer, in a readable form, an account of the physical features of Ireland, and of the economic and social activities of its people. It deals therefore with matters of fact rather than with matters of opinion; and, for this reason, it has happily been found possible to avoid political controversy. Ireland deserves to be known for her varied scenery, her wealth of archæological and antiquarian lore, her noble educational traditions, and her literary and artistic achievements. The progress and status of Ireland as an agricultural country are recognised and acknowledged, but her industrial potentialities have, until recently, been inadequately studied. The causes of the arrested development of her industries have been frequently dealt with. Her industrial resources, however, demand closer attention than they have hitherto received; their economic significance has been enhanced by modern applications of scientific discovery and by world-wide economic changes. It is hoped that these pages may contribute to the growing movement in the direction of industrial reconstruction.

It is unusual to enlist the services of many writers in a work of modest dimensions, but it was felt that the more condensed an account, the more necessary was it

to secure authoritative treatment.   It is hoped that the
names of the contributors will afford a sufficient guarantee
that the desired end has been achieved.   The editorial
task of co-ordinating the work of these contributors
has been made light and agreeable by their friendly
co-operation.

The scope of the volumes and the mode of treatment
adopted in them suggest their suitability for use in the
higher forms of secondary schools.   A notable reform
is in course of accomplishment in the teaching of geography.   The list of place-names is making room for the
more rational study of a country in relation to those
who dwell in it, and of these dwellers in relation to their
environment.

G. F.

DUBLIN, *November 1st*, 1921

CONTENTS

ILLUSTRATIONS

ILLUSTRATIONS

MAPS AND DIAGRAMS

Geological Map of Ireland . . . . Front Cover

The Mourne Mountains 13
The River Erne 17
Map of Ulster (500-foot contour) 20
Map of Ulster (250-foot contour) 21
The Londonderry Area 23
The Belfast Area 24
Pelophila borealis, Distribution of . . . 98
The Giant's Ring, Drumbo 115
Plan of Dundrum Castle 135
Physical-Political Map of Ulster . . . End of book

Available for download from www.cambridge.org/9781107511422

The illustrations on pp. 11, 16, 26, 31, 33, 35, 38, 41, 43, 45, 48, 51, 144, 145, 153, 155, 166, 167 are reproduced from photographs by Valentine & Sons, Ltd.; that on p. 28 from a photograph by Mr W. A. Green; those on pp. 59, 79, 110, 121 from photographs by Mr R. Welch; the sketch-maps on pp. 115, 135 are reproduced by permission of the Royal Society of Antiquaries of Ireland; the illustration on p. 138 from a photograph supplied by Mr F. J. Bigger; that on p. 136 by permission of Lord Walter Fitz-Gerald; the portrait on p. 172 is reproduced from the painting by G. F. Watts by arrangement with Emery Walker, Ltd.; the portrait on p. 174 is from a painting by John R. Dicksee in the Nat. Gallery, Dublin; and that on p. 176 from a daguerrotype.

Acknowledgments are due to the Department of Agriculture and Technical Instruction for Ireland, and to the Royal Irish Academy for permission to use illustrations which have appeared in their publications.

ULSTER

ANCIENT GEOGRAPHY

THE oldest source of information that we possess regarding the ancient geography of Ireland is contained in the work of the second-century Alexandrian Ptolemy.

The following are the geographical names which he preserves for us in Ulster. The *Okeanos Hyperboreios* or " Northern Ocean " washed the northern shore of the island. Into this projected three promontories, called respectively *Boreion Akron*, *Venniknion Akron*, and *Robogdion Akron*—probably corresponding respectively to the Bloody Foreland, Malin Head, and Fair Head. There are five tribes mentioned by Ptolemy as occupying the region now called Ulster. These are the *Venniknioi* in the north-west ; the *Robogdioi* in the north-east ; the *Erdinoi* south of the first named ; the *Darinoi* south of the second ; and the *Volountioi* south again of the last. The Volountioi had a city, *Regia*. These are certainly the " Ulidians," who gave their name to the province, and their city may have been *Emhain Macha*, the royal seat of the northern kings. The *Erdinoi* are by name and position equated to the Erna of Irish history. The name of the Robogdioi has been ingeniously compared to Roboc, the traditional name of an aboriginal chieftain compelled by a later invader to servile labour, according to the *Book of Invasions* : as these Robogdioi were established in the place where the native traditions put

the Pictish aborigines, Roboc may well have been one
of their tribal names. Ptolemy also mentions the
mouths of the following rivers ; in the west, the *Ravios*
or Erne ; in the north, dividing the Venniknioi from
the Robogdioi, the *Vidova*, probably a copyist's mistake
for *Vilova* or Foyle ; and the *Argita*, which from its
position must be the Bann : in the east, the *Logia* or
Lagan, and the *Vinderis*. The last-named has not been
identified ; from its position it must have been somewhere near Newry.[1] Somewhere north of the mouth
of the Boyne was *Isamnion*, which may have been either
a cape or a town : its identification is uncertain.

The modern name Ulster, like Leinster and Munster,
is a hybrid, consisting of the suffix -ster (Icelandic *staðr*=
a steading), added to the old name Ulaidh. Like most of
the ancient territorial names in Ireland, this was originally the name of a population, not of a tract of land.
Originally the *Ulaidh* occupied the whole of what is now
called Ulster—that is, the part of Ireland cut off by a
line joining the mouth of the *Drobhas* (now the Drowse,
at Bundoran in Co. Donegal) with *Inbher Colptha*, the
mouth of the Boyne. After A.D. 332, however, the
name lost its extended application, and the Ulidians
proper were restricted to the lands east of the River Bann,
Lough Neagh, and the Newry river ; that is, the modern
counties of Antrim and Down. A very mixed population inhabited this region, with a large infusion of the
aboriginal element, called *Cruithne* in Irish history—
the same race as is usually spoken of as the Picts. The
district was further subdivided among a number of

---

[1] It is barely possible that the name is a corruption (due to a
lapse of memory on the part of Ptolemy's informant) of *Ceann-
tragha*, the old name of the site of Newry.

ancient septs, as the *Dál Riada* in North Antrim, the *Dál n-Araide* in South Antrim and North Down, and the *Dal Fiatach* in South Down. It appears that the kings of Ulidia (in this restricted sense) were selected alternately from the Dal n-Araide and the Dal Fiatach.

The remainder of the modern province of Ulster was divided as follows. In the central portion was the great territory of *Tír Eoghain*, the Land of Eoghan—the territory of the tribe claiming descent from Eoghan (died A.D. 465) son of Niall of the Nine Hostages (king of Ireland A.D. 379-405). The peninsula between Lough Swilly and Lough Foyle bears his name (Inshowen, *i.e.* Inis Eoghain, the island of Eoghan). The western part of Donegal bore the name *Tír Chonaill*, the land of Conall—the territory of the reputed descendants of Conall Gulban, another son of Niall, died A.D. 464. The remnant of the *Airghialla* occupied the south of the province—in Louth, Armagh, Monaghan, and Fermanagh. They had originally occupied the whole of Central and Southern Ulster, but were dispossessed from Tir Eoghan at the beginning of the fifth century.

On the coming of the English, Ulster was granted as a *palatinate* (that is, a territory the administrator of which had sovereign powers delegated to him), to De Courcy. It was afterwards re-granted by King John to the De Lacys. No success, however, attended their efforts to extend the powers of England in this province, which, till the Tudors, remained the least amenable of the five to English authority. Some time before the reign of Edward II. counties called Antrim, Down, and Louth had been formed, the last-named at the time being counted to Ulster ; but no other counties were made till the end of the sixteenth century. As a preliminary to the extension of English jurisdiction over the whole province, after the rebellion of the O'Neills, the limits of the modern counties of Donegal, Fermanagh, Cavan (till then counted to Connacht), Coleraine (now Londonderry), Armagh, Tyrone, and Monaghan were laid down by Sir John Perrott; but the troubles in the province prevented the final establishment of the division till about 1610.

The wholesale confiscations and compulsory colonisation of Ulster by aliens, under the reign of James I., has had a permanent effect on the population of the province. Already, as we have seen, there was a considerably mixed population within it, as the aboriginal Pictish inhabitants were very largely represented here; probably in a greater proportion than in the other provinces. The Anglo-Normans did not make any very great upset in the balance of the elements of the population. This was reserved for the early Stuarts, who, in order to save themselves further annoyance from this troublesome province, deported its eastern inhabitants to the barren lands of the west, and settled its rich plains with colonists from Scotland and England. The descendants of these settlers remain to this day. The distribution of the colonists varies greatly. In Antrim they form about 75 per cent. of the population; in Cavan they are not more than about 20 per cent; in the county of Donegal they are practically non-existent.

POPULATION

No observations of the physical anthropology of Ulster have ever been taken, and it is therefore impossible to give any details of the mixed multitude that forms the population of this province. The stronghold of the

Irish language in the province is Donegal, the Irish of which has, as might be expected, many points of resemblance to Scottish Gaelic. The census returns of 1911 show an advance in the number of Irish speakers ; even of those who could speak Irish only the number rose from 4456 in 1901 to 4737 in 1911. The total number of Irish speakers was in 1891 84,152, or 5.2 of the population of the province ; in 1911, it was 96,440, or 6.1 of the population. Most of the counties showed a rise, except Cavan (a county that is much depleted by emigration).[1] Thus Antrim rose in the twenty years from 894 to 2724 ; the city of Belfast from 917 to 7595.

TOPOGRAPHY

ULSTER occupies the northern fourth of Ireland. No general, well-marked lines form its demarcation from Leinster and Connaught (on which it abuts on the south), such as the line of the Shannon, which separates the two last-named provinces from each other. On its eastern edge, indeed, the frontier of Ulster is guarded by the barrier of hills which separates Newry from Dundalk, and which culminates in Slieve Gullion (1893 feet). But elsewhere the boundary is unmarked by outstanding physical features. Starting on the Atlantic shore in Donegal at the Drowse river, which separates Donegal from Leitrim for a few miles, it traverses Lough Melvin, a large and pretty lake, and follows the valley south-east through Kiltyclogher to Lough Macnean, where Co. Cavan comes

[1] 10.7 per cent.—3.2 per cent. higher than any other of the Ulster counties.

in on the northern side. Turning south through the
mountains, it almost reaches Lough Allen, and runs
thence over the top of Slievenakilla (1793 feet), on
through the low lake-strewn country to near Carrigallen,
where Leitrim gives place to Longford, and the provinces
of Ulster, Connaught, and Leinster meet. The line
meanders on across the mazy Lough Gowna to Lough
Kinale, where, for a few miles, Westmeath fronts Cavan
across the open expanse of Lough Sheelin. The boundary
then lies between Cavan and Meath as far as Kingscourt,
its general direction now changing from south-east to
north-east. Monaghan now replaces Cavan on the
northern side, and faces Meath for a few miles and then
Louth. On the Leinster side Louth continues the
boundary to the sea, but on the Ulster side Armagh
replaces Monaghan. The country again becomes
mountainous for some miles, and the boundary line
reaches tidal water at Narrow-water, on the shallow
inlet which runs from the head of Carlingford Lough
to Newry. Thence to the open sea Carlingford Lough
forms the boundary, where the Mourne Mountains
look across to the high serrated ridge of Carlingford
Mountain.

Nine counties are included in the province, notes on
which will be given later. They have a total area of
8566 square miles. This area is exceeded by Munster
(9536 square miles), and itself exceeds that of Leinster
(7619), and Connaught (6802).

The province offers a remarkable variety of types of
surface and scenery, due to the variety of rocks of which
it is built up. A line drawn from Magilligan Point in
Co. Derry to Portadown, and thence to Belfast, cutting
off the north-eastern part, defines roughly the basaltic

area, which forms a high, well-marked plateau of wide
moors overlooking the eastern coast, and a less well-
marked upland in the west.   It is depressed in the centre,
where a broad, fertile valley runs northward to the
sea from Lough Neagh, whose waters escape down this
trough.   The line which marks the southern limit of
the basalt, if prolonged S.E. to the boundary of Connaught, forms the northern edge of a great area of slates,
which occupies all the country southward save for the
granite areas around Carlingford Lough.   This slate
country is hummocky, fertile, and highly tilled.   Another
line drawn westward from Lough Neagh to Donegal
Bay roughly defines the boundary of the large area of
granite and metamorphic rocks which prevails over the
north-west, and of the region of limestones and other
rocks of the Carboniferous period which form south-
western Ulster.   The types of surface in these areas
reflect the structure and composition of the underlying
rocks : in the north-east the plateau is deeply covered
with peat ; its coast-line is precipitous and extremely
picturesque ; the lower grounds are highly fertile.   The
slate area, as stated above, is hummocky and fertile.
The N.W. area of schists etc., is mountainous and wild,
with great ridges running N.E. and S.W.   The Carboniferous area is very varied, as in many places masses of
shales and sandstones overlie the limestone floor, and
produce abrupt changes in the characters of surface and
soil.   Taken as a whole, Ulster is a hilly but fertile area.
The only large stretch of low or flattish ground lies
around Lough Neagh and thence northward down the
Bann valley to the sea.

The Ulster climate has the characteristic features of the
Irish climate in general—that is, it is cooler in summer

and warmer in winter than most areas situated within
the same latitude ; it has a heavy rainfall and a
perennial humidity. The coldest winters in Ireland
(below 40° F., average in January) are found in an oblong
area stretching from the central part of Ireland almost
to the north-east coast : this area includes most of Ulster
except Donegal ; there the winter temperature is higher,
western Donegal being above 42° F. in January. The
coolest summers in Ireland are found in the coastal
regions of northern Ulster, where the average July
temperature is as low as 58°. The annual rainfall may
be roughly said to be below 40 inches in the eastern half
of the province, and above this in the western half, the
precipitation increasing to over 50 inches (probably
exceeding 60 in some of the mountainous parts) in the
western half of Donegal, where also the effects of the
prevailing westerly winds are felt in a peculiar degree.

MOUNTAINS

The largest area of high land is in the north-west, in
Donegal and Tyrone ; but the loftiest summits lie in
the south-east, in the compact upland of the Mourne
mountains. The following mountain groups may be
distinguished, though in the north-west the highlands
are almost continuous.

Donegal is strongly folded from north-east to south-
west, and erosion along the axes of folding has given
rise to rocky ridges and deep valleys. The highest
points amid a sea of hills are Muckish and Errigal (2466
and 2197 feet respectively) far to the north-west.
Muckish is a heavy, rather featureless dark ridge ; Errigal
a beautiful cone of white quartzite, which contrasts with
the dark hills by which it is surrounded. The low-lying

lakes around its base tend to enhance its height, and add greatly to its beauty.

Immediately to the south of the ridge which contains Errigal and Muckish, the Derryveigh mountains form a massive ridge culminating in Slieve Snacht (2240 feet). A short distance south of this upland lies the deep and romantic Glen Veigh, which occupies part of the most remarkable of the N.E.-S.W. valleys of which mention has already been made. These ridges and valleys cross Lough Swilly into the peninsula of Inishowen, where another Slieve Snacht rises to 2019 feet. Far to the south, the group of the Blue Stack mountains or Croaghgorm reaches 2219 feet.

The strong folding to which Donegal has been subjected has a marked effect on human life within the area. Traffic naturally lies along the troughs which run northeast and south-west ; the construction of roads or railways in directions more or less at right angles to this is fraught with difficulties, as the successive ridges offer serious obstacles. The effect is to cut off the northwestern portion of Donegal from free communication with other parts of the country. The coastal district, which is strongly indented in the direction of the folding, though very irregular in surface, is generally low, and comparatively level roads join the heads of the many bays and inlets, where most of the villages are situated. Good roads also traverse the valley troughs ; but from the fertile district of the Foyle basin, lying south of the hill-area, only a very few roads and a single railway find their way, by many windings and steep climbs, across the wave-like succession of heathery ridges.

A high bare east-and-west ridge of mica-schist, the Sperrin mountains, rises on the borders of Derry and

Tyrone, attaining 2240 feet in Sawel.   For twenty miles
or more, on almost every side of this central mass, hills
rise, stretching to the Swilly valley on the west and the
Bann valley on the east, and overlooking Lough Foyle
on the north.   Two of the most conspicuous of the
outliers of this mass are Slieve Gallion on the south-
east, which looks down on the Tyrone coal-field and
Lough Neagh, and the beautiful cliff-walled hill of
Benevenagh on the north, which rises imposingly above
the great sandy flat of Magilligan, at the entrance of
Lough Foyle.

The basaltic plateau of Antrim and Derry has been
alluded to already.   The highest points are in the north-
east of Antrim, where Trostan and Slievenance form flat
domes rising to 1817 and 1782 feet respectively.   Further
northward, Knocklayd forms a fine isolated dome of
1695 feet.   The basaltic hills impend over Belfast to a
height of over 1500 feet.   The hills thus form a kind of
broken rim to the basaltic area, on the eastern side
running from Ballycastle southward to Larne, and thence
along Belfast Lough to Lisburn, and on the western side
south from Magilligan to the more ancient ridge of the
Sperrin mountains.   A broad fertile basin lies between
the two edges.   The upper part of the basin has sunk so
far as to become flooded, and Lough Neagh, the largest
extent of fresh water in the British Isles, 153 square miles
in area and generally only 40 to 50 feet in depth, is the
result.   The lower part of the basin accommodates the
outlet stream from Lough Neagh—the Lower Bann—and
is a rich and well-wooded area with many busy linen
factories.   Along the Antrim coast, the exposed edges
of the basalt and underlying Mesozoic rocks have been
carved into deep romantic glens.

Glenariff, Co. Antrim

Plateau-basalts overlying Mesozoic Strata

Glenariff, the most famous of these, is 4 miles long and 1000 feet deep, with a flat alluvium-filled bottom towered over by lofty cliffs. Good modern roads traverse all these valleys, crossing the boggy plateau at their heads at elevations of over 1000 feet, and dropping down the gentler reverse slope of the hills to the fertile basin behind.

A beautiful group of granite hills rises in the southern portion of Co. Down, stretching from Newcastle to Carlingford Lough. Slieve Donard (2796 feet) is the culminating point, and over a dozen peaks exceed 2000 feet. The slopes are steep and rugged, with deep picturesque valleys. The main mass of mountains, which lies east of the road that crosses from Hilltown to Kilkeel (the only road traversing the range, and rising at its highest point to 1225 feet), consists of a compact horse-shoe-shaped string of high domes, with a second line of peaks running down the centre of the horse-shoe : thus forming two main valleys, down which run the Annalong and Kilkeel rivers. The latter has cut a magnificent glen : its waters are drawn off near the lower end for the supply of Belfast. Here and there the granite forms lofty cliffs, hung with grasses and ferns, and fantastic pinnacles, cut across by horizontal joints, so that they resemble towers formed of huge boulders built up one above the other. The granite is extensively worked into kerbs and square-setts, and in many places the clink of the stone-dressers' hammers mingles with the murmur of the streams. Except near Newcastle and Rostrevor, where the hills descend steeply into the water, a sloping plain several miles wide, studded with cottages, lies between the highland and the sea.

South and west of the Erne valley down into Leitrim,

where Ulster gives place to Connaught, there is a large
mass of hilly ground, much of which, however, lies out-

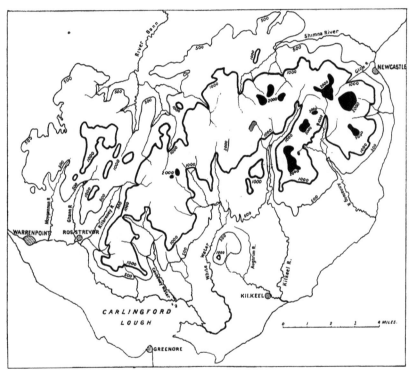

The Mourne Mountains

side the boundaries of the province with which we are
at present concerned.

The most northern of these uplands, that lying be-

tween Lower Lough Erne, Lough Melvin, and Lough
Macnean, is wholly in Ulster.   Round the flanks of this
mass rise a number of picturesque precipitous limestone
hills.   In the north, Shean North (1135 feet) looks down
on Lough Erne in a noble cliff which forms the most
striking feature of the lake shores.   Near by, to the west
of Church Hill and Derrygonnelly, there is some very
picturesque country, with limestone cliff-walls, little
lakes, and deep wooded glens.   The great semi-circular
precipice of Knockmore is specially worthy of mention.
Further south again, Belmore Mountain presents a tall
range of cliffs.   In the centre of the area, behind these
hills, and resting on the limestone, massive beds of sandstone are spread, producing a quite different kind of
surface.   The beds are tilted towards the north, and
display on that side a series of parallel low precipitous
scarps, with a long dip-slope running back from each to
the next scarp.   The rain, working down these slopes,
has formed a series of long, narrow lakes, where it has
collected at the foot of the scarps.   The change from
the hilly limestone country, with its grey rock and green
grass, to the broad, dark moorland, crossed by these long
waves of sandstone, is most striking.

Between Lough Allen and Upper Lough Erne a higher
range lies, culminating in Cuilcagh (2188 feet), which
runs out in a long, cliff-edged ridge to Tiltinbane
(1949 feet).   Four miles southward a parallel ridge runs
from Benbrack (1648 feet), to Slievenakilla (1793 feet).
Between the two ridges, which are joined at the eastern
end, a wide mountain valley extends which forms the
head-waters of the Shannon.   Tradition makes the
source of the river a deep round pool, called the Shannon
Pot, which forms the exit of an underground stream, a

small tributary of the main stream, known as the Owenmore. This underground stream comes, presumably, from Eden Lough, a mile to the eastward, which has no visible outlet, though a stream from the summit of Tiltinbane flows into it.

RIVERS AND LAKES

The most extensive river system in Ulster is that of the Bann. This stream rises in the Mourne mountains at the southern end of Co. Down, and flows north-westward for some thirty miles through Banbridge and Portadown, and past many linen factories to Lough Neagh, which it enters near its south-western corner. A few miles further westward, an equally large stream also enters the lake—the Blackwater, which drains a large part of Monaghan and Tyrone, and flows northeast. Other streams flow into the lake from east, west, and north. The combined drainage leaves Lough Neagh at Toome, in the north-east corner, and passing through the shallow and hardly distinct Lough Beg, flows northward as the Lower Bann down the wide central trough of the basaltic area, already alluded to, to reach sealevel at Coleraine, and the sea itself four miles lower down. A feature of this trough is that down the centre runs a low ridge. The northward-flowing Bann occupies the western of the two valleys thus created. In the eastern, only five miles from the Bann, the River Main flows for 25 miles parallel to it but in the opposite direction, to enter Lough Neagh below Randalstown. As described in a paragraph on Canals (p. 25), the Upper Bann, Blackwater, and Lower Bann are all used as waterways.

Next to the Bann, the Erne, draining south-western Ulster, is the largest river in the province. It is a strange stream, a great part of its course being occupied by lake-expansions filled with such a multitude of peninsulas and islands that without a guide, or close attention to a good map, it is hardly possible to find one's way by boat.   The course of the Erne lies mainly through a broad, low limestone valley, and most of these expansions are due to solution of the rock by water.

The River Bann at Coleraine

This explanation will not, however, account for the formation of the lake in which the river has its origin—Lough Gowna in Longford, which lies on slate rocks, and represents a piece of submerged " drumlin " country ; drumlins are the whale-backed mounds, due to glacial accumulation, and they prevail over much of the slate region. From Lough Gowna the river flows through Lough Oughter in Cavan, and then passes into Upper Lough Erne, a very maze of land and water, and past Enniskillen

to Lower Lough Erne, which is larger and more open,
being 18 miles in length and up to 226 feet in depth.   At

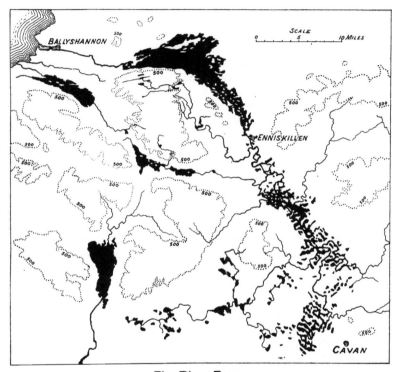

The River Erne

Belleek, at the lower end of this sheet of water, the Erne
at last loses its lake-like character, and plunges down
through a beautiful gorge to the sea below Ballyshannon.
   In contrast to the Erne, which consists mainly of a

u B

chain of lakes, with slow, placid reaches between them, the Foyle, which drains most of the northern part of central Ulster, is a much-branched river-system without lakes, and with a rapid flow in all its branches. The main stream rises on the hills round Fintona in Tyrone, and flows northward (as the Strule river) to Omagh, where it receives a tributary from the east, the Camowen river. Thence (as the Mourne river) it runs on, receiving the Derg from the west, to Strabane, where it is joined by a tributary almost as large as the main stream, the Finn, which drains much of eastern Donegal. Below Strabane it becomes tidal, and (as the Foyle) flows north-eastward, broad and with muddy banks, for 18 miles past Londonderry to the sea at the head of Lough Foyle.

The Lagan, chiefly known from the fact that Belfast is built on its banks, is quite a short stream, rising on Slieve Croob, in the centre of Co. Down, and flowing first north-west and then north-east through Dromore and Lisburn to Belfast, where it enters Belfast Lough.

The Shannon is the only river which belongs in part to each of the four provinces of Ireland. Its birthplace is claimed by Ulster. The spot which is traditionally pointed out as its source is a deep pool in which an underground stream, carrying some of the drainage of Tiltinbane, in N.W. Cavan, comes to the surface (see p. 14). After a course of a few miles the infant Shannon crosses into Connaught.

Lough Neagh, the largest sheet of fresh water in the British Isles, occupies 153 square miles in north-east Ulster, and is bordered by five out of the nine Ulster counties—Antrim, Down, Armagh, Tyrone, and Londonderry. It is squarish in shape, and curiously uniform in depth, the bottom being a flat plain, 40 to 50 feet below surface, save at the north-west corner, where a deep cut, sinking to 102 feet below the surface, occupies the the centre of the short arm which leads to the overflow channel (the Lower Bann), at Toome. The shores are not much indented, and islands or reefs are rare. Drainage operations in the early part of the nineteenth century lowered the level of the lake by several feet, and have in most places left a wide, stony foreshore. The depression which forms Lough Neagh is due to a sinking of the central part of the basaltic plateau of N.E. Ireland, which also produced the wide valley through which the waters of the lake escape northward to the sea.

The string of lakes—Lough Oughter and Upper and Lower Lough Erne—which form rather than interrupt the course of the River Erne, has been briefly described already when dealing with that stream (p. 15). Less than Lough Neagh, Lower Lough Erne is larger than any other lake in Ulster.

The province is abundantly supplied with small lakes, particularly in Donegal, and on the slate area which extends across Down, Armagh, Monaghan, and Cavan.

TRAFFIC ROUTES

The courses of roads, railways, and canals are determined by two main considerations—the desirability for passing close to the towns, whose needs they are designed to serve, and the necessity for avoiding, so far as possible, obstacles such as hills. Canals are the most sensitive to surface features, on account of the cost of the construction and upkeep of locks, and the time lost in passing them ; roads are the least sensitive. But it is by a study of the railways that the connection between surface features and traffic routes is best seen, because canals are too few and roads too many to reflect the conditions prevailing. In Ulster, uplands—areas of, say, 500 feet or more—are of frequent occurrence and wide distribution. The only extensive area of low land is

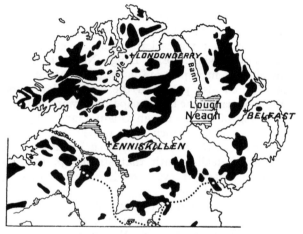

Map of Ulster (500-foot contour)

the Lough Neagh basin in the east and its outlet towards the north ; the western portion of the province especially is much diversified. A glance at the map on p. 21, which indicates the 250-foot contour, will show that from the Lough Neagh basin four depressions radiate towards north, south, north-east, and south-west ; all of these are occupied by both railroad and canal. West of this system, an almost unbroken upland sweeps from Lough Foyle down to Upper Lough Erne. This tends to isolate

Londonderry which lies behind it, and which is reached from Belfast by circuitous routes. The direct distance between these towns is 68 miles, but by the Midland Railway we travel 95 miles, and by the Great Northern 100 miles to get there. In south-western Ulster, the valley of the Erne provides a useful highway, which is

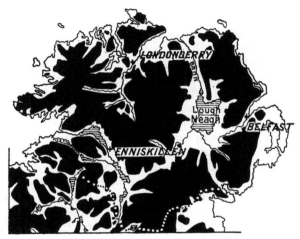

Map of Ulster (250-foot contour)

also utilised by railways throughout its length. The valley-system of the Foyle, running south from Londonderry, much assists the railway in its passage through the hilly country of Tyrone.

The main line from Dublin to Belfast, rising from sea-level at Dundalk, enters Ulster by a steep climb (1 in 100) through a pass in the mountains which fill the promontory between Carlingford Lough and Dundalk Bay. Thence it follows a convenient depression northward to Portadown on the River Bann, a few miles from Lough Neagh. Turning eastward, it crosses a low watershed into the valley of the Lagan, and reaches Belfast without difficulty. An important branch of the same line runs north-westward from Dundalk, across the hummocky surface of Co. Monaghan to Clones, whence it proceeds to Enniskillen, utilising the Erne valley, a branch following that river to the sea at Bundoran. The line to Londonderry keeps on northward, and, crossing a low watershed into the Foyle basin, follows the rivers Mourne and Foyle through Omagh and Strabane. The establishment of a connection from Belfast, *via* Portadown, to Derry was more difficult, as it involved the crossing of the Tyrone barrier mentioned earlier. To surmount this the line rises to 650 feet near Pomeroy, dropping then into the Foyle basin, and joining the branch from Dublin (referred to two sentences back) at Omagh.

Competitive railway routes are rare in Ireland, but an example exists between Belfast and Derry. The Great Northern, as we have seen, avoids the main mass of the Tyrone-Derry highlands by sweeping round to the south. The Midland Railway (formerly the Belfast and Northern Counties, now the Midland, Northern Counties Committee) goes northward, and reaches Derry by way of the coast. At the outset, this route is blocked by the Belfast hills, which form a high north-east and south-west ridge, passing close to the city. This obstacle is passed by running northward between Belfast Lough and the hill-slopes to Greenisland (whence a branch proceeds through Carrickfergus to Larne), and then turning sharply back and climbing westward across the divide (325 feet elevation) between Carnmoney Hill and The Knockagh. Thence an easy route leads through Antrim

and Ballymena to Coleraine; the line here crosses the
River Bann where it becomes tidal, and turning westward, pursues a level course along an old raised beach,
overhung in places by high cliffs, to Derry. Between
Castlerock and Downhill, the old beach has been washed

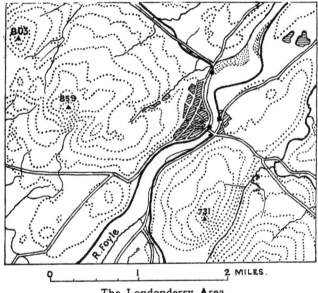

The Londonderry Area

away, and the line has to tunnel through a projection of
high ground, where the waves beat against the cliffs.
The line has several branches running towards or into the
hilly country on either hand, and on the eastern side
narrow-gauge lines connect with Larne, Parkmore, and
Ballycastle; the terminus at Parkmore lying on the top
of the basaltic plateau at an elevation of over 1000 feet.

The Belfast and County Down Railway connects Belfast, Downpatrick, and Newcastle (37 miles) with branches to Bangor, Newtownards and Donaghadee, Ballynahinch, Ardglass, and Castlewellan. It runs over hummocky country formed of Silurian slates, and serves a rich agricultural district and several seaside resorts.

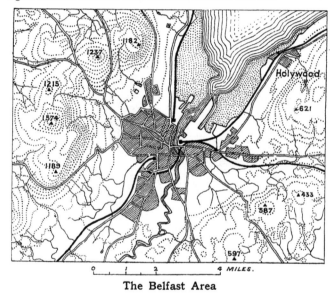

The Belfast Area

From Derry and Strabane on the River Foyle, narrow-gauge lines lead far into the adjoining mountainous region of Donegal. The Londonderry and Lough Swilly Railway, winding among the hills, and passing through much beautiful scenery, eventually reaches Burton Port, on the remote western coast; a branch runs northward to Buncrana and Carndonagh, on the peninsula of Inishowen. Another line, the Donegal Railway, runs westward through Strabane, and forks at Stranorlar, one branch keeping westward to Glenties, while the other climbs through the mountain gap of Barnesmore (600 feet), and, descending to sea-level, runs through the town of Donegal to the busy little port of Killybegs. A branch leads southward from Donegal to the Great Northern system at Ballyshannon.

The canal system of Ulster has its centre in Lough Neagh. From Belfast a waterway leads to that lake up the River Lagan, and thence by an artificial cut across a very low divide to the lake. Two waterways leave the south end of the lake; one utilises the Upper Bann to a point beyond Portadown, and continues along a narrow deep depression past Goraghwood to Newry. Thence to the sea near Warrenpoint, the canal is much broader and deeper, so that steamers can discharge their cargoes at Newry. The other waterway runs from the south-west corner of Lough Neagh, and utilises the River Blackwater for some miles; continuing south-west, it reaches the River Erne near the head of Upper Lough Erne, whence it continues to join the Shannon Navigation near Carrick-on-Shannon. From the north end of Lough Neagh to the sea at Coleraine the Lower Bann has been canalised.

Large areas in Ulster are unsuitable for canal construction, and are devoid of waterways.

ROUND THE COAST

Carlingford Lough, across which Ulster faces Leinster, is a lovely inlet set round with mountains. The town of Warrenpoint stands near its upper end, beyond which a narrow, shallow inlet, now with a ship-canal on its southern bank, leads up to Newry. The village of Rostrevor, beautifully situated in a very sheltered corner, nestles on the eastern shore. From Carlingford Lough the Co. Down coast sweeps in a wide curve round to Belfast. On the way, Newcastle, a well-known holiday

Newcastle and Slieve Donard

resort, is passed. North of the shallow bay of Dundrum a narrow, deep channel leads into the land-locked Strangford Lough. This is an island-studded basin running north and south for a distance of 20 miles. It averages about 4 miles wide, and is separated from the Irish Sea by a tongue of very fertile land (the Ards) of about the same breadth. The outer shore of the Ards is the most easterly part of the Irish coast. It is low, and on account of its projecting position and its dangerous outlying reefs, is more prolific of shipwrecks than any other portion of the shores of Ireland. North of the Ards the town of Donaghadee, once used as a mail-packet station in conjunction with Portpatrick on the Scottish coast, is passed ; also the Copeland Islands, and then Belfast Lough is reached. This forms a safe anchorage, and is a busy thoroughfare on account of the position of Belfast at the head of it. Carrickfergus, which was a place of note when Belfast was a fishing village, stands on the northern shore, guarded by its ancient castle, and Bangor, an important residential adjunct of Belfast, on the southern. North of Belfast Lough, Island Magee forms a peninsula similar to the Ards, but higher and smaller, enclosing the quiet waters of Larne Lough. The outer shore of Island Magee presents an imposing cliff-wall of basalt. At the outlet of Larne Lough stands the busy town of Larne, whence a " short-sea " passenger service is carried on with Stranraer, the distance being 35 miles.

From Larne northward to Fair Head and on eastward to Portrush, where Antrim joins Derry, the coast-line is remarkable for its boldness, and for the contrasts of colour which its cliffs and scarps present. The black of the basalt is set off by the pure white of the Chalk, and ruddy sandstones and marls and blue-grey Lias clays enhance the effect. A raised beach, forming a narrow platform between the cliff bases and the sea, has allowed of the construction of a fine thoroughfare from Larne to Cushendall, one of the most picturesque roads in Ireland. Fair Head presents a magnificent face of giant basaltic columns, facing across to the Mull of Kintyre, distant only 13 miles ; further eastward the great cliff-walls which overlook the famous Giant's

Causeway exhibit a series of successive beds of lava, which form an epitome of the volcanic history of the country in Cainozoic times. The Causeway itself is one of these beds, in which very slow cooling has resulted in a splitting up of the homogeneous rock into polygonal columns. Several little towns lie along the coast;

" Pleaskins," Giant's Causeway

Portrush and Ballycastle, in the north, are the most important, and are both well-known summer resorts. Rathlin Island, a cliff-bound outlier of the basaltic plateau, rises out of the waves a few miles to the north of Ballycastle. On the eastern part of the coast lie Cushendall, Carnlough, and Glenarm.

Beyond Portstewart, a few miles east of Portrush, the River Bann enters the sea between areas of sand-dunes; it is tidal and navigable for steamers as far as Coleraine,

5 miles up. East of the Bann the great triangular sand-flat of Magilligan, a raised beach of comparatively recent date, almost blocks the entrance of Lough Foyle, with the lofty basaltic cliffs of Benevenagh looking down on it.

Lough Foyle is a large triangular land-locked inlet.

The Coast Road near Glenarm

It is mostly quite shallow, but a channel leads along the northern (Donegal) shore to Londonderry, situated on the Foyle, 5 miles above the point where the river debouches into the head of the lough. Londonderry is well placed on a hill overlooking a bend of the river.

Westward of the mouth of Lough Foyle, the coast of Donegal at once assumes the wild, romantic aspect which characterises it throughout. Round the edge of Inishowen, the large peninsula enclosed between Lough Foyle and Lough Swilly, wild headlands and tall cliffs alternate with sheltered sandy bays and great boulder beaches. Malin Head, at the extremity of the peninsula, is the most northerly point of the Irish mainland ; but the islet of Inishtrahull lies several miles further north. The deep and picturesque inlet of Lough Swilly, 25 miles in length, winding far to the southward through the hills, forms a spacious and safe harbour, and presents much beautiful scenery ; the little towns of Buncrana and Ramelton stand one on either side of its waters. Beyond Lough Swilly there is a tangle of land and water, Mulroy Bay being exceedingly complicated in outline, Sheep Haven being more open. This district is a favourite one for tourists. West of Sheep Haven, the lofty promontory of Horn Head stands boldly out, its towering cliffs overhanging the ocean to a height of over 600 ft.

Beyond Horn Head a long stretch of rocky, much-indented coast-line, mostly low in elevation, with high hills inland, runs south-west for some 40 miles in a direct line (twice or three times as much if measured along the shore), to Loughros Bay. Many islands lie off the coast, the most important being Aran (not to be confused with the Galway Bay Aran or the Scotch Arran), and Tory. The latter lies far out, 7 miles from the nearest point of the mainland, and is still a very primitive place, but well provided with fine fishing-boats. Much fishing is done all along this coast. Towns are very few and small ; a narrow gauge line, winding through the bogs and rocks, connects this remote region with the main traffic routes at Londonderry.

Slieve League, from Malinbeg, Co. Donegal

Forming the most westerly portion of the Donegal coast, the high bare Malinmore promontory, cliff-bound and mountainous, presents much bold scenery. Beyond its extremity, where lies the little island of Rathlin O'Birne, the coast at length trends eastward, and we pass under the tremendous cliffs of Slieve League, 1972 ft. in height, into Donegal Bay and a softer type of scenery. The busy little town and harbour of Killybegs provides a sheltered anchorage, and a narrow-gauge line runs eastward to join the Great Northern Railway at Ballyshannon and Strabane. Long, low projections of limestone run far into Donegal Bay, and at its shallow upper end is the little town of Donegal. Thence the coast trends south-westward to the sandy mouth of the River Erne, where stands the town of Ballyshannon, and a few miles further on, close to the point where Donegal joins Leitrim, and the province of Ulster the province of Connaught, we reach the pleasant watering-place of Bundoran.

COUNTIES AND TOWNS

Ulster has an area of 8566 square miles, and is divided into nine counties as follows :

	Area in Square Miles.	Population.
Donegal .	1,870	168,537
Londonderry .	816	140,625
Tyrone .	1,260	142,665
Antrim .	1,191	480,016
Down .	957	305,098
Armagh .	512	120,291
Monaghan.	500	71,455
Cavan .	746	91,173
Fermanagh .	714	61,836
Total .	8,566	1,581,696

Slieve League, from above Roxborough, Co. Donegal

u C

Of these, Donegal, Derry, Antrim, and Down lie on the coast, and the other five counties inland, Armagh just touching tidal waters.

Co. Donegal

Donegal is the most northerly county in Ireland, and extends along much of the north-west coast. It is a large area, and filled with mountains and valleys with a strong N.E. and S.W. trend. The coast is much indented. The rivers are short. Nearly one-third of the total area is barren mountain land.

Towns are few, and lie mostly in the south and east, which is the lower and more fertile portion. Ballyshannon (2170), at the mouth of the River Erne, is a busy place, as is Letterkenny (2194) on the River Swilly, a few miles above the head of Lough Swilly ; Killybegs (1634), far to the south-west, has a good natural harbour and an important fishing industry ; Lifford (419), on the River Foyle, may be looked on as a suburb of Strabane, on the opposite (Tyrone) side of the river ; Buncrana (1848) is a favourite seaside resort. Londonderry itself, though on the Donegal side of the Foyle, belongs administratively to Co. Londonderry.

Co. Londonderry

This is another hilly county, but it has a belt of low cultivated land along the northern side, where it fronts Lough Foyle, and along the east, where lie the valley of the Bann and Lough Neagh.

Londonderry (40,780), one of the most important and historic towns in Ulster, stands in the extreme west of the county, in a commanding position on a bold hill looking down on a curve of the Foyle, here a broad tidal

Londonderry

river. The main part of the city stands on the northern or Donegal side of the stream, but the county boundary swings northward so as to include it and its environs. The town is bright and busy, with good buildings, and the quay accommodation is ample. There are four railway stations, two on either side of the river. The walls of the old city, which run round the hill which forms the middle part of the town, are still in an excellent state of preservation. Five miles below Londonderry the river widens out into the broad expanse of Lough Foyle.

Coleraine (7785), on the River Bann where it ceases to be tidal, is also a port, and is an important place. Limavady (2667) lies half-way between the last two. Kilrea (783) is on the River Bann, which for a long distance forms the boundary between Derry and Antrim. Maghera (872), and Magherafelt (1233), lie towards the southern end of the county.

Co. Tyrone

Tyrone is a large hilly county, occupying the north-central part of Ulster. On the north-eastern edge the ancient ridge of the Sperrin mountains rises to 2240 ft., and heathery hills continue southward right across the county. The only low ground is along the Lough Neagh shore on the east, and the valleys of the tributaries of the Foyle, which drain the greater part of the county, in the north-west. There is a larger amount of tillage and a smaller area of grass than the Irish average. There is a coal-field around Dungannon and Coalisland in the east, which is worked in a small way.

Strabane (5107), in the north-west, is a busy town standing where the River Finn joins the Mourne to form the Foyle. Omagh (4836) is situated on a tributary of the Foyle in the centre of the county. Dungannon (3830) and Cookstown (3685) lie to the east, not far from Lough Neagh, the former perched picturesquely on a steep hill.

Co. Antrim

Co. Antrim forms the north-east corner of Ireland, and includes the nearest point of approach to Great Britain, the channel which separates Fair Head from the Mull of Kintyre being only 13½ miles in width. The strait is very deep, and a strong tide sweeps through it. The eastern two-thirds of the county are hilly, with wild heathery moorlands dropping sharply into the sea, and forming a magnificent coast-line ; the western third is occupied by the low and fertile valley of the Bann and Lough Neagh.

Belfast (386,947), the second city in Ireland and the principal centre of industry, owes its position to the ford which formerly existed near the site of the present Queen's Bridge : its rapid growth is of quite recent date. The central parts of the town are built on ground raised but slightly above high-water mark, and formed of soft clays laid down by the sea when the land stood lower than at present. As a consequence, the principal buildings are all " on stilts "—they rest on series of long piles driven through the soft deposits to harder ground underneath—sometimes as much as 40 ft. below the surface. The city has essentially a modern aspect ; and by far the handsomest building—the City Hall—was finished only a few years ago. The Municipal College of Technology is a fine building near by ; the Queen's University stands in the southern suburbs. Most of the other larger buildings are warehouses and factories. There are

three railway termini. The Great Northern Railway runs
south-west up the Lagan valley to reach Dublin, Cavan,
Bundoran, and Londonderry. The Midland Railway
trends north-west, to serve Co. Antrim and Co. Derry ;
and the Belfast and County Down Railway runs south-

City Hall, Belfast

east through Co. Down. Branch lines serve the residential places on either side of Belfast Lough.

The famous shipyards stand on both banks of the
river, below the spacious docks. Although coal and iron
occur but in limited quantity in Ireland, the proximity
of Belfast to the mining areas of Scotland and the North
of England allows of their easy import in quantity. The
old winding channel of the Lagan has been straightened
and deepened at great expense. Belfast has a large

cross-channel traffic. Passenger steamers run nightly to Fleetwood, Liverpool, Heysham, Ardrossan, Greenock, and Ayr. A considerable part of the city stands on the eastern or Co. Down side of the river. The situation of Belfast is particularly fine. A high range of basaltic hills looks down on it on the western side, and on the opposite side of the fertile and well-wooded valley of the Lagan rise the lower, cultivated hills of Co. Down. Immediately below the city, Belfast Lough extends, 12 miles in length by 3 miles or more in breadth, forming a fine anchorage sheltered from all quarters save the east.

Lisburn (12,388), on the Lagan, and Ballymena (11,381), on the Main in the middle of the county, are important centres of the linen industry. Larne (8036), at the entrance of Larne Lough, has also large manufactures, and is one terminus of the " short-sea " route between Ireland and Great Britain, the other being Stranraer, distant 35 miles by water. Carrickfergus (4608) was a place of importance when Belfast was a fishing village ; it is a quiet little town, dominated by its Norman castle. Portrush (2107), in the extreme north-west, is a large and rising watering-place. Ballycastle (1485) and Glenarm (951) are also on the sea ; Ballymoney (3100) and Ballyclare (3369) are inland.

Co. Down

Co. Down is a low, fertile and singularly hummocky area. Two-fifths of it are under crops—an unusually large proportion. The continuity of its small well-tilled fields is broken by the fine group of the Mourne mountains (2796 ft.) in the south, the lower upland of Slieve Croob (1755 ft.), in the centre, and by the large land-locked expanse of Strangford Lough in the east. The coastal parts, though low, are very pretty. In the extreme south, the Mourne mountains descend into the Irish sea and Carlingford Lough, providing beautiful scenery about Newcastle, Warrenpoint, and Rostrevor. The Lagan, rising on Slieve Croob, flows across the county and then along its northern edge to Belfast. The Bann rises in the Mourne mountains and runs north-west to Lough Neagh.

Towns and villages are scattered thickly over the county. Newry (11,963) lies in a deep valley in the south, connected with Carlingford Lough by a ship canal. Banbridge (5101) is an important centre of linen manufacture ; Newtownards (9587), at the head of Strangford Lough, specialises in muslin weaving. Bangor (7776) and Donaghadee (2213) in the north, and Newcastle (1765) and Warrenpoint (1938) are much frequented seaside resorts. Downpatrick (3199), the assize town, is an old and quiet place. Ballynahinch (1667) is an important market town in the centre of the county. A portion of Belfast (Ballymacarrett) lies in Co. Down, having a population of 100,795.

Co. Armagh

The same drift-covered, hummocky Silurian rocks which prevail over Co. Down continue south-westward across Armagh, Monaghan, and south Cavan into Longford, and produce the same type of surface and scenery, low, rolling, and fertile, with many small steep, cultivated hills, and little lakes gleaming in the hollows. It is only in the extreme south, where granite rocks prevail, that the surface attains any considerable elevation (Slieve Gullion, 1893 ft.). In the north, where the county fronts Lough Neagh, large bogs are

found. Here the Upper Bann passes through Portadown to Lough Neagh. The north-western boundary
is the Blackwater, used as a canal in the lower
portion.

Armagh, the county town (7356), is a very ancient
place, and has a quiet dignity about it. The visitor will

Protestant Cathedral, Armagh

be struck with the prevalence in the buildings and
pavements of red marble, which is quarried locally.
Armagh is the metropolitan see of all Ireland, and has
two cathedrals. Lurgan (12,553) and Portadown (11,727),
in the north-east, have considerable manufactures connected especially with the linen industry. The former
is an important railway junction. In the south-east,
part of Newry belongs to Co. Armagh.

Co. Monaghan

This county, which adjoins Armagh on the south-west, resembles it in respect of size, shape, and surface, except that the highest ground is in the north-west (Slieve Beagh, 1221 ft.), and that the county does not border on Lough Neagh. Like Armagh, it is highly tilled, with undulating Silurian rocks in the south and flatter limestones in the north. Considerable rivers are absent, but small lakes are very numerous.

Monaghan (4272), the county town, lies in a narrow depression which connects the Lough Neagh and Erne basins, and carries the main road, Great Northern Railway, and Ulster Canal in a south-west direction to Clones (2401). The latter town, an early ecclesiastical centre, stands boldly on the top of one of the little round hills which are so numerous on the Silurian area, from Co. Down to Co. Cavan. Carrickmacross (2064) in the south, and Castleblaney (1692) and Ballybeg (2961) in the centre, are bustling market towns.

Co. Cavan

Cavan, adjoining Monaghan on the south-west, is a larger and more diversified county than either of the last two, with a long arm running north-west into the Sligo-Fermanagh highlands. A continuation of the north-eastern slate area covers the main part of the county; limestone and Coal-measures form the uplands in the north-west. Across the middle of the county the River Erne flows northward, forming a strange tangle of land and water (p. 17). It spreads out in Lough Gowna in the south of Cavan, and Lough Oughter in the centre; these lakes are a mere maze of points, bays, and islands. Elsewhere lakes of all sizes are abundant. The highest

The Diamond, Monaghan

Rossmore Castle, Monaghan

point of the mountainous N.W. portion is Cuilcagh
(2188 ft.) on the Fermanagh border. Near here the
Shannon has its source.

Cavan, the assize town (2691), stands near the middle
of the county ; Cootehill (1550) in the north-east, and
Belturbet (1371) among the lakes of the Erne valley, are
busy towns ; the latter has connection by water down
the Erne and by the Ulster Canal to Lough Neagh, etc.

Co. Fermanagh

Co. Fermanagh may be said to consist of the lower
part of the Erne basin. That river winds slowly across
the area, forming the large island-filled expanses of
Upper and Lower Lough Erne, so that no less than one-
ninth of Fermanagh is under fresh water. The upper
lake in particular is a mere maze of channels, peninsulas,
and islands. Away from the water-logged valley, much
of the county is hilly, and the scenery often highly
picturesque, especially in the Derrygonnelly district.
The highest point is Cuilcagh (2188 ft.) on the borders
of Cavan ; and the south-western boundary is full of
hills and lakes.

Enniskillen (4847), built on an island in the Erne
between the two great lakes, is much the most important
town. It is a bright, busy place, with good shops and
public buildings. The other towns in the county are all
small, but many are good market centres, serving large
tracts of fertile country. The village of Belleek, at the
western end of Lower Lough Erne, is well known for its
pottery, which possesses a peculiar creamy glaze.

Enniskillen, from Portora

GEOLOGY

TABLE OF FORMATIONS FOUND WITHIN THE PROVINCE

Cainozoic Group

System	Chief Types of Irish Rocks.
Post-Pliocene	Drift deposits.
Pliocene .	?
Miocene and Oligocene	Absent.
Eocene . .	Basalt lavas of north-east Ulster, Gabbro of Louth and Mourne granite.

Mesozoic Group

Cretaceous .	White limestone of Antrim and Londonderry.
Jurassic . .	Oolites—Absent. L. Lias—bluish or dark shales. Rhætic—dark shales and "White Lias."
Triassic . .	Keuper— Red marls with rock-salt at Carrickfergus and gypsum at Carrickmacross. Bunter—Red Sandstones of Lagan and Dundonald valleys.

PALÆOZOIC GROUP

Permian — Breccias at Armagh; Magnesian limestone near Cultra, Co. Down.

Carboniferous:
- Coal Measures / Millstone Grit — Sandstone and shales with seams of coal in upper series.
- Carboniferous Limestone — Limestones and shales.
- Carboniferous Shale — Sandstones with coal at Ballycastle.

Old Red Sandstone — Conglomerates and red or mottled sandstones.

Granite of Newry and Donegal.

Silurian / Ordovician — Sandstones and shales.

Cambrian — Absent.

Pre-Cambrian — Metamorphic rocks (gneisses, mica schists, quartzites, etc., in Donegal, Londonderry, Antrim, and Tyrone.

The rocks which compose the crust of the earth may be divided into two groups—*aqueous* or *sedimentary* and *igneous*. Aqueous rocks were laid down in water whilst igneous rocks have cooled from a molten state. Both types may be altered by heat, pressure or crustal movement, and are then termed *metamorphic*.

Sedimentary rocks, though laid down in water as horizontal layers or beds, may afterwards become tilted or thrown into folds by pressures in the crust, which may themselves be the result of the solidified envelope accommodating itself to a shrinking interior.

Glencolumbkille, Co. Donegal

Scenery of the Metamorphic Region

Rocks tilted at various angles may be seen in quarries and cuttings. Sometimes in a quarry or other section, beds are seen to be curved in the form of an arch or *anticline*, or the curve may be of an opposite character forming a trough or *syncline*. Occasionally, too, a series of beds may be seen having an inclination or *dip* in one direction followed above by another series with an entirely different inclination. The explanation of this is that the lower series were laid down as flat sheets then tilted up forming dry land. The agents of denudation—rain, frost, etc., reduced this land surface, and depression followed, allowing the upper series to be deposited upon the upturned edges of the former.· Elevation again occurred ,and this was again followed by denudation. In such a section the rocks above are said to be *unconformable* with the series below, but the members of each series are conformable amongst themselves. In other words, an unconformity indicates a break in the sequence of the beds or *strata*. As is readily understood the lower beds in a quarry section are the older and the upper ones the younger, except where overfolding has taken place or where under exceptional stresses the rocks have become dislocated and masses of older rock have been thrust bodily over rocks of more recent age.

Some idea of the time taken to form a bed of rock may be gauged by observations of the rate at which deposits of a similar nature are now being formed in our seas and rivers, but there are so many factors to be taken into account, that these attempts at a time scale are only roughly approximately correct.

Referring now to the table, we see that the stratified rocks are divided into three groups and the words

u D

employed in naming these—Palæozoic, Mesozoic, and Cainozoic—refer to the types of animals that lived in these times as determined from the remains of their harder parts, which we term *fossils*.

In the Palæozoic era animals altogether different from those of to-day inhabited the seas, and in the latter part of it dominated the land as well. The Mesozoic era gave birth to animals that had certain resemblances to those that had previously existed in the Palæozoic, though in other features they resembled those that came into existence in the Cainozoic era; whilst in the most recent group, at its beginning, the mammals appeared in large numbers and many varieties, and included amongst them the early ancestors of the domesticated horse.

The rocks of these groups are further subdivided into systems such as Carboniferous, Triassic, etc. These have subdivisions, and so we get down to what we started with —the individual beds.

It will be observed that in the list of our Irish rocks there are very large blanks. These are filled up in Great Britain or on the Continent.

Emerging from beneath rocks of much later formation, we find highly altered sand and mud rocks—quartzites and mica schists—to which the local term Dalradian has been applied, after Dalriada, the old name for the north-east of Ireland, where some of these rocks occur. They may be seen down on the shore of Murlough Bay, whilst north of Lough Erne between Pettigo and Ballyshannon, they are found over a wide stretch of country. In Donegal, Londonderry, and Tyrone are large tracts of metamorphic rocks which must be classed amongst the oldest in the country. They include quartzites such

Clady River and the Quartzite Cone of Errigal

as are exposed on the sharply sculptured peaks of Errigal
and Muckish mountains, mica schists and gneisses which
make up the bulk of the Sperrin mountains, and the
highland area of Tyrone.

A belt of Ordovician and Silurian rocks consisting of
shales and sandstones runs in a north-easterly direction
from Cavan to the Co. Down coast. In the latter
county, these rocks form the uplands to the south of
the Lagan valley. Across the North Channel they are
again exposed in Wigtonshire and run north-eastward
to the shores of the North Sea. In the early part of the
period represented by these rocks a sea studded over
with islands occupied the area that is now Ulster. In
Tyrone, limestones are found interbedded with lavas
and ashes which are thought to have been erupted in
Ordovician times. We know, too, that volcanic activity
was displayed then in other parts of Ireland, notably in
counties Kildare, Dublin, and Waterford.

At the close of Silurian times the crust was lifted up
and anticlinal and synclinal folds were formed. In
connection with these " Caledonian " foldings, molten
masses of granite were brought up from below and became consolidated at some depth below the surface in
Donegal and about Newry. Subsequent denudation
has revealed these, and they now appear as mountains
or highlands with axes running north-eastwards. Desert
conditions prevailed over this newly-made land ; and on
plain, in delta, and in lake, sands were accumulated.

The constituent particles of these rocks are held together by a cement of iron oxide, and to this material
is due the warm colour that distinguishes them. In the
country between Omagh and Enniskillen we find an extensive outcrop of these Old Red Sandstone rocks. Farther

north on the western shore of Lough Swilly is another, but smaller exposure of these red rocks.

The beginning of the Carboniferous period saw most of Ulster once more submerged beneath the sea. In the deeper waters to the south limestones were formed, while in the shallower northern part sands and muds accumulated. Evidently the shore of the Carboniferous sea was not far to the northward, for in the neighbourhood of Dungiven and Fivemiletown, and along the eastern border of Tyrone, beach deposits or conglomerates were formed, whilst at Lough Eask, in Donegal, sandstones were deposited at a time when limestones were being formed only a few miles to the south.

Deltas soon made their appearance at the mouths of the rivers which entered this sea, and upon these a luxuriant vegetation sprang up. Forests flourished and decayed, and as the deltas upon which they grew subsided, they were covered by water and sands were piled up over them, and so by slow degrees they were converted into coal seams. The north Antrim coal seams are of earlier formation than those of England, but present features comparable with the seams of Scotland, where coal was being formed at a time when limestones were being deposited in the deeper waters that lay over the centre of England. Coal of this early age is found east of Ballycastle, whilst seams of later formation and similar to the English type occur at Coal Island, near Dungannon. Sandstones occur in the district south of Lough Foyle, also in a belt bordering the limestone not far from the town of Donegal, and in patches in Tyrone; while limestone is developed in the northern parts of Armagh, Monaghan and Cavan, and over a considerable area in Fermanagh. In Fermanagh, and

in the Cuilcagh district, we have representatives of the
Millstone Grit series, which, by their resistance to the
action of the weather, have preserved the softer shales
and limestones below in the hills of Cuilcagh and Slieve
Beagh.

Ulster suffered in the general uplift that followed
upon the close of Carboniferous times, and large areas of
Coal Measures were swept off the surface by denudation.
After much had been removed, a depression set in which
admitted the sea to a portion of the north-east of the
province.   In this Permian sea the magnesian limestones
of Cultra, Co. Down, and of Tullyconnel, Co. Tyrone
were formed, and also the red breccias near Armagh city.

With the beginning of the next period, the sea had
again retreated, and under desert conditions the red
sandstones of the Lagan and Dundonald valleys and
of Carrickmacross were laid down.   In the latter part
of this period certain lakes dried up, and the salts
contained therein were deposited from solution.   Gypsum is found at Kingscourt and Belfast, while at Carrickfergus salt deposits of considerable thickness occur in
the marls.   On Scrabo Hill near Newtownards, a thick
covering of later basaltic lava has preserved the red
sandstones in which may be seen sun-cracks, ripple-
marks, and pitted surfaces, the latter indicating hollows
made by rain drops on the damp sands.   These were
afterwards baked by the heat of the sun during a period
of recession of the shore line, and when the surface of
the lake or sea was again extended, fresh deposits of
sand covered and preserved them.

Gradually the sea again covered a considerable portion
of the north-east of Ulster, and in it shales which are
considered to form passage beds from Trias to Lias

strata were laid down. These graduate upwards into the blue Lias shales which are found in many places round the edge of the Antrim plateau occupying a position immediately under the " white limestone." It is the presence of these shales that is responsible for the landslides occurring so commonly about Glenarm and at other places on the Antrim coast.. The limestone above is porous, and besides this it is traversed by large cracks or joints, and water percolating through the rock or finding its way along these joints reaches the impermeable shales below. The upper layer of these shales becomes changed into mud and forms a lubricated surface. If now the dip of the strata in a valley side or sea cliff is towards the valley or the sea, a landslide of a block of limestone, separated from the main mass by a large joint, is the natural consequence.

We do not know how long this early Jurassic or Liassic sea remained, nor can we tell how much more than now remains of the Lias strata was laid down, but eventually dry land appeared once again, and probably remained during the times in which thousands of feet of oolitic limestones were being formed in the south of England. It was only at the end of the Cretaceous period that the sea returned in full strength, and then our chalk, with layers of flint disposed in bands at intervals, was developed as a limy ooze. A considerable percentage of this ooze was composed of minute shells of lowly organisms, called foraminifera, whose size was no greater than that of the head of a pin. After frost these tiny shells can be scraped off from weathered surfaces of limestone with a knife, and their form, and sometimes their structure, can be determined by the aid of a lens or microscope. Chalks were thus laid down over the north-east of Ulster and are now found emerging from underneath the basalt rock from near Lurgan to Belfast and round the Antrim coast to Portrush, and in the eastern part of Londonderry.

An uplift raised these freshly formed chalks above

Fair Head, from Murlough Bay

Pre-Cambrian Rocks in foreground, Carboniferous Sandstone on the shore below the cottage, Basalt in the promontories beyond

the sea, denudation followed, and a rolling country, much like the Downs of the south of England to-day, was the result.

Then a great change came over the scene. Volcanic energy that all through the Mesozoic era had slumbered now awoke, and in Antrim and the adjoining counties,

from great cracks in the crust there issued lavas that
swept along the valleys filling them up. These fissure
eruptions continued at intervals until the country was
buried beneath two or three thousand feet of lava at

The Castles of Commedah, Mourne Mountains

*Undetached pillars are formed by weathering along the vertical
joints*

least. Though most of the lava came to the surface
along great fissures, yet there were a few centres such as
Carnmoney north of Belfast, Slemish near Ballymena,
and Carrick-a-rede on the north coast of Antrim, that
may very properly be described as the sites of volcanoes.
In Carrick-a-rede may be seen the huge blocks that

were shot up out of the crater only to fall back again into the volcano, and be cemented together once more as solid rock. Intrusive igneous rocks—gabbros—were formed in Louth, contemporaneously with the earlier basalts of Antrim, and these have weathered out into rough and rugged forms which are well displayed in Carlingford Mountain and Slieve Gullion. Later, the Mourne granite came into being, consolidating below the surface from the molten condition about the time when eruptions of acid lavas—rhyolites—were ejected in the vicinity of Tardree, five miles north-north-east of Antrim, and in other places at intervals during the prolonged period which separated the earlier from the later basaltic eruptions. The Mourne granite presents to-day a series of peaks, characterised in general by smooth dome-like surfaces, which contrast strongly with the serrated character of the gabbros on the one hand and the plateau features of the basalts on the other.

In the times between the basaltic eruptions vegetation quickly spread over the soil derived from the easily decomposing lavas. Trees grew up, and were overwhelmed in the succeeding lava flow. This wood was then attacked by waters containing silica, which material replaced the woody fibre, particle by particle, and so the petrified wood, commonly found along the shores and in the waters of Lough Neagh, was formed ; not by any petrifying action of its waters, but by replacements that took place some millions of years ago.

During Eocene times the climate was more tropical in character, and in these inter-basaltic periods, the surface of the lava decayed in much the same way as rocks do now in tropical countries where seasonal rains

are experienced. The products of this decay of the
Antrim lavas are exemplified in the iron and aluminium
ores which occur in a zone separating the earlier from
the later eruptions. This zone is well shown in the red
band that is seen half-way up the cliffs at the Giant's
Causeway (see p. 28). Here, too, we have good examples

Basaltic Cliffs of Benevenagh, Co. Londonderry

of the symmetrically formed columns which have
been evolved by shrinkage during the cooling of the
lavas.

The effect of the pouring out of such a quantity of
lava on the chalk was considerable. It became a hard
limestone. The flints, too, that lay about on the surface
and in the beds of the streams were penetrated by the
waters containing iron solutions, and we find them trans-

formed into red or variegated jaspers, thus bearing
testimony to their contact with the molten stream.

After the eruptions had ceased, a subsidence took place
in the lava surface and into this hollow the drainage
of the highlands naturally emptied itself and formed
an earlier Lough Neagh.

A long period of denudation now intervened before
the advent of glacial times during which much of the
upper basalts were removed, and the main features of
the topography of Ulster were carved out.

In one area at least we have reason to believe that
a considerable alteration in the drainage system took
place before glacial times. About two miles east of the
Foyle is the river Faughan which runs parallel with the
former river for a few miles and then the parallelism is
maintained for 9 or 10 miles further by the Burngibbagh
valley, down which a stream flows to join the Faughan.
Both valleys are mature in form and there is nothing in
the structure of the rocks to account for this parallelism.
As there is no indication that the upper Faughan ever
crossed the present watershed to join the Foyle, the
Burngibbagh is considered to have been the original
main river, having the upper part of the Faughan as a
tributary. Its head waters appear to have been diverted
into the Foyle, which, though unimportant in the
beginning of its history, yet cut back its valley much
more rapidly than did the main river, and so gained
its present predominance.

THE GLACIAL PERIOD

The climate that in Eocene times had been sub-
tropical became colder until, at the beginning of the
Glacial Epoch, the conditions were somewhat like

those in Spitsbergen to-day. Snow accumulated in the uplands, and was compacted into glaciers which issued forth upon the lowlands. Scotland was heavily glaciated, in some places perhaps to a depth of 4000 or 5000 ft. From its southern highlands fields of ice were thrust out, filling the North Channel and invading the coasts of Antrim. The general trend of this ice was south and it eventually reached the open sea through St George's Channel.

Information concerning the motion of glaciers is obtained in various ways. Rock surfaces are found which are smooth and polished by the sand held in the base of the ice, and often grooves and striations are made upon them by the stones similarly held. The striations indicate the line along which the glacier has travelled but do not always show the direction from which it came. Sometimes projecting masses of rock have one side smoothed and the opposite side craggy, and then it is plain that the polished side opposed the motion of the glacier. Erratics can often be traced to their place of origin, and are thus useful in determining the movement of the ice that carried them.

By carefully working out the details of facts such as these in various localities in Ireland, the Rev. Maxwell Close, who was the first to study the glaciation of the country systematically, arrived at some interesting conclusions regarding it. He found that in Ireland there were two distinct glaciations—one of a general character which was the heavier, followed by another that was of a more local nature. The greatest precipitation of snow in the earlier cycle of glaciation was along a zone extending from North Galway to Lough Neagh. Glaciers were given off from this region towards the south, north, and west, and rode over the country regardless of the smaller local irregularities, and only affected by the more extensive elevated regions, which nourished their own snow-fields and opposed their

Granite Erratic resting on Slate, Rostrevor, Co. Down

This large block of Newry Granite was carried southwards to its present position by the ice stream

glaciers to the advancing streams, thus diverting them to some extent.

In the Belfast district, the general trend of the ice was south-westward from the basalt highland, but between Bangor and Newtownards it took a more southerly direction. Near the city of Londonderry, two sets of striations occur, one running west-south-west,

and a prevailing later set running north or north-east.
The former of these must have been made by ice coming
from the east-north-east, for in addition to striations a
brown boulder-clay is found with fragments of basalt,
chalk, flint and red sandstone, the parent masses of
which occur some 15 miles to the east. The later

Esker at Creggan, 10 miles west of Cookstown, Co. Tyrone

glaciation appears to have been from the south and
south-west, for the drift contains amongst other materials
red granite from Barnesmore, some 30 miles to the south-
west. In the Silurian tracts of Monaghan and Cavan
the striations indicate a south-easterly trend of the ice,
whilst from the highlands of Fermanagh ice streams
were sent forth towards the sea at Donegal Bay.

With the introduction of a milder climate the glaciers

diminished in size, and as they melted, boulder-clays were left behind upon the surface. The form of these varied in different localities. In some places they were spread out in broad sheets and in others where the surface was broken by rocky hummocks, as in the Co. Down, they were accumulated in rounded " drumlins," producing what is commonly described as the " basket of eggs " type of topography. At Creggan in Tyrone, some 10 miles west of Cookstown, meandering gravel ridges occur in great profusion. These owe their origin to streams that flowed under the ice, and may, perhaps, mark the place where such streams, during the period of retreat of the ice-sheet, dropped their burden of sand and gravel where they encountered standing water. A similar small esker occurs in the Lagan valley and is easily traced from Brookmount through Lisburn to Dunmurry.

It will readily be understood that the conditions existing during the retreat of the glaciers greatly affected the drainage systems. Ice remained in Belfast Lough when the lower part of the Lagan valley was free, and here a lake was formed which extended westwards beyond Lisburn. The stratified clay deposits of this lake are now used for brick-making in some of the yards to the east of the Lagan. This lake may have had an outlet to Strangford Lough by way of the Dundonald valley. When the ice obstruction finally disappeared the Lagan did not resume its old channel, but sought the sea over the lowest part of the drift surface by a course which lies to the east of the old bed.

About 3 miles to the east of Londonderry is the small glen of Fincairn. This gorge is 100 ft. deep and about two-thirds of a mile long, and has a level bottom. This

must have been an overflow channel begun at a time
when the Faughan valley had 250 ft. of ice in its bed,
thus obstructing the drainage in that direction.

The curious steep-sided pools that are met with in
the gravels and sands on the right bank of the Foyle

Kettle-hole, two miles N.E. of Londonderry

north of Londonderry, mark the places where lobes of
ice became separated from the main body of the glacier.
Sands and gravels were deposited over and around
them, and afterwards when melting took place, these
kettle holes, as they are called, were formed.

At the close of the glacial period the land was higher
than now, for we have, in addition to the geological
evidence, that of the relict fauna and flora, for believing

that a land connection with Norway remained after that with the Continent by way of France was broken. Then came a depression that allowed the sea to re-enter certain of the river valleys of the north. Carlingford Lough was thus invaded, and Belfast Lough extended farther to the west than now, and the estuarine clays on which the lower part of Belfast now stands were laid down. An old shore line can be traced from Belfast round the Antrim and Londonderry coasts, showing that at this time the sea stood some 25 ft. higher than it does to-day. Afterwards, an uplift occurred that brought the sea to its present position and exposed the stumps of ancient forest trees and the peat of formerly submerged bogs.

Old records and tradition point to the fact that Inishowen was, up till very recently, an island, separated from the mainland by a narrow strait that joined Loughs Foyle and Swilly along the line of the present Lough Swilly railway. Farther south, the low tract from Blanket Nook to Carrigans suggests the probability that the tract to the north was similarly cut off. Inch island retained its insular character till quite recently, when the shallow strait was reclaimed from the sea by artificial embankments ; and the hill upon which the city of Londonderry was built was an island in the Foyle until, by the building of walls on the south-west and north, the sea was kept out of what is now the valley to the west of the old city.

SOILS

In many places in Ulster the soils are not formed by the decay of the rocks that underlie them, but owe their presence in the places where they are found to the transporting agency of ice. In the hilly tracts and in scattered patches in other places, soils are, however, formed *in situ*.

In Donegal and Down are large areas of granite, which yield a poor sandy soil, deficient in plant food, the potash in the form of carbonate, which results from the decomposition of the felspar, having been carried away in solution.

Basalts give strong rich clays, with a considerable amount of lime and some phosphoric acid.

Limestone soils are often shallow and warm, and yield a very nutritious vegetation. Some limestones yield a small percentage of phosphoric acid, and the soils formed from them are in consequence greatly enriched. Soils derived from limestone are sometimes deficient in lime, for this is removed as a bi-carbonate, and only the clayey impurity of the lime is left.

Silurian grits and shales yield soils which vary according to the predominance of one or the other rock. Where sandstones are in great abundance, the soils are usually fine, and vegetation thrives.

Metamorphic rocks—gneisses, mica-schists and quartzites—are found over large areas in Donegal, Londonderry, and Tyrone ; and associated with the gneisses and quartzites in these counties are tracts of barren lands.

The province has benefited largely by its inheritance of ice-borne or drift soils. In Donegal débris from altered shale (mica-schist) rocks, with some limestone occasionally included, has been deposited over granite, and patches of good soil are formed along the western coast. Around Donegal and Upper Lough Erne the soils owe their richness to the limestone débris of the boulder-clay, but about Ballintra a sandy drift covers a limestone area and the soils are poorer in consequence. South-west of Londonderry the drift is of considerable thickness, and the soils are fertile owing to the variety of the materials from which they are derived. About Omagh we have again a rich assortment of different rocks in the drifts—grit, limestone, basalt, and altered slate. In North Antrim glacial sands and gravels cover extensive areas, and bogs have been formed in the depressions between the mounds. In the south of the country is the fertile valley of the Lagan. This, as Sir R. Kane pointed out, owes its fertility to the commingling of different kinds of rocks. To the north of the valley is the basalt escarpment, with limestone immediately below. On the south rises the Silurian highland with grits and slates, while the valley itself is carved out of Triassic sandstone, and over the whole we have a greater or less depth of boulder-clay, the materials of which have come from the north-west. The Dundonald valley is similarly fertile, for it too is carved out of red Trias sandstone, and is bounded on either side by Silurian strata, while the drift contains basalt and white limestone débris.

In Armagh and Down, sands and gravels have a wide distribution, whilst in the southern parts of Armagh, Cavan and Monaghan, the Silurian area has been greatly enriched by the limestone drifts.

MINES, MINERALS, AND QUARRIES

Mining for Iron ore (Hæmatite) is largely confined to Antrim. The deposits occur in the interbasaltic zone, which in many places, as at the Giants' Causeway, is coloured a brilliant red. Basalt contains a considerable percentage of iron usually in the form of magnetite, and the iron ores may be considered as a decomposition product of the rock which then formed the surface.

The conditions of climate that obtained in the period between the outpouring of the lower and upper basalts differed from those now existing in being more tropical in character. In tropical India, Africa, and South America, where there is seasonal rainfall a decay is brought about in rocks and forms soils and subsoils, the materials of which are very similar to those observed in the red interbasaltic zone. It is highly probable that the deposits in Antrim were similarly produced.

The deposits are chiefly hæmatite, which is often pisolitic or pea-like in structure. Mining has been carried on in many places, more particularly in the vicinity of Claggan near Parkmore and Glenarm. It is near these two places that active mining is in progress now. The ore from the Glenarm area is shipped direct from Glenarm in small vessels. In 1910 the export from here was 15,000 tons. From the Parkmore mines the ore is carried by light railway to Ballymena, and thence by the Midland to Belfast, whence it is shipped to England. In 1910, 51,000 tons were dispatched along this route. Hæmatite also occurs in the Slieve Gallion district in Tyrone.

Bog iron ore (Limonite) is formed by the action of bacteria and also by accretion from water round tiny shells of diatoms. These on dying, fall to the bottom and form a sort of spongy mass. Its finely divided form enables it to take up sulphur and other impurities readily, and it is thus used for the purification of gas and afterwards becomes more valuable as a source of sulphur and ammoniacal salts. This ore is found in many parts of Donegal especially around Rathmullen and Malinmore. Ore is dug at these two places and exported.

Bauxite occurs in the red zone in connection with the iron ores. In some places, the bauxites are derived from Rhyolite (a lava of the granite family of igneous rocks), as at Glenarm and Straid, under conditions similar to those that gave rise to the iron ores. In other places it occurs in a fluviatile deposit, it having either been washed down into the lower parts of the valleys as a mud, or been carried by the wind. Four companies are working the bauxite deposits. Most of the ore is obtained from the Ballintoy district.

In the Aluminium works at Larne, aluminium hydrate is produced by the action of caustic soda on powdered bauxite in presence of a small amount of aluminium hydrate. The hydrate is calcined and then sent to Foyers, on the Caledonian Canal, for smelting by electricity. In 1910, over 6000 tons of bauxite and 10,000 tons of alumina were exported. Formerly the Antrim ores were exclusively used, but now an increasing quantity of French ore is imported.

Salt occurs in the vicinity of Carrickfergus, Carrickmacross and Kingscourt in the upper Triassic. The salt accumulated on the old lake bottoms from which the waters were evaporating. Hollow-faced cubes of hardened clayey material are found in the brick clays at Belfast and Moira. These are pseudomorphs of salt crystals the original material of which had been removed by solution. The salt is obtained from the mines by dissolving the mineral and pumping out the brine, which is then evaporated. In Cork city the waste heat of lime-kilns is sometimes used for the evaporation of brine. The " Tee " process, by which the salt is purified by fusion, has been recently introduced by the International Salt Co. In 1910, 7500 tons were exported from Belfast and 13,500 tons from Carrickfergus.

Gypsum, like salt, is found as a product of dessicating lakes of Triassic times. Veins of gypsum occur in the brick clays of Belfast, and large deposits are found at Carrickmacross, one seam near this place being about 60 ft. thick.

Prospecting for lead ore is being carried on near Keady, and galena occurs in many places in Monaghan. At Conlig, near Newtownards, are old lead mines.

Felspar was found in sufficient quantity, and of sufficient purity near Belleek to admit of its being used in the preparation of pottery there. Afterwards, white and black mica impurities increased so much that it was rejected in favour of pure felspar imported from Norway.

Diatomaceous earth is a siliceous vegetable deposit. It is found at various places—Toome, Portglenone, and Kilcrea,—along the banks of the lower Bann. The material is dug, and when dried like peat is white in colour. It is then powdered by machinery and used as an insulator.

Steatite or Soapstone is used in the preparation of French chalk. It is mined at Lough Gartan, Churchill, Co. Donegal.

The coal series at Ballycastle resembles the Scotch more than the English type of formation. Several seams may be observed in the cliffs between Ballycastle and Fair Head. Mining has been carried on at intervals in this field. At present, however, the output is small and sufficient to supply only a limited local demand.

In Tyrone is the only field which offers much scope for the prospector, for it is very probable that here the Coal Measures dip under the Triassic sandstones to the east. The coal is of the bituminous type and occurs in thick seams. One of these, the Annagher seam, is 9 ft. thick. Deposits of fireclay and coal are being worked in the vicinity of Coal Island. Lignite is found at Sandy Bay on the eastern shores of Lough Neagh.

The Coal Island district is the only one in Ireland where true fireclay occurs, and here fireclay and sanitary goods are manufactured. There seems, too, to be a prospect of a fuller development of this industry. The district is connected with Belfast by rail, and a canal runs to Lough Neagh, from which lake goods can easily be distributed to various centres, also by canal.

Limestone of Cretaceous age and white in colour is obtained all round the edge of the basaltic plateau of Antrim. It is not used as a building stone, but lime is made in many kilns and this is used for building purposes, and also as a top-dressing on land. The southern side of the Lagan valley which has no limestone is thus supplied from the kilns on the north, of which there are many between Moira and Belfast. The lime used formerly to be carted for considerable distances ; now most is sent by rail. Lime-burning is an important industry at Cookstown, Clones, Belfast, Larne, etc. Whiting is made in some lime works, and is shipped from Belfast to England. The flint which occurs in thin beds in the White Limestone was formerly discarded by quarry owners. Lately, however, a demand has arisen for it in connection with poultry farming, poultry requiring grit as an aid to digestion. The flints are ground up and sold in grades of varying degrees

of fineness. Flint is also used in pottery making, and
a considerable quantity of this material is sent from
Ballycastle to the Potteries.

At Magheramorne, a large Portland Cement factory
has recently been built. The raw materials are White
Limestone, dredgings from the lough, and a shale which
is obtained in the neighbourhood.

Clay suitable for brick-making is found in great
abundance in the vicinity of Belfast, in the Triassic
strata which lies under the basalt-limestone escarpment;
and also on the eastern side of the Lagan, where yards
are worked in glacial deposits and " warp " clay, which
latter represents a glacial lake deposit. In the larger
works, the clay is mixed and the bricks moulded by
machinery, and burning is done in " continuous " kilns.
The best bricks are made from the Glacial clays, and
from these are also made terra cotta mouldings, drain
pipes, tiles and chimney pots of the best quality. At
one time it was a common practice when building houses
on clayey ground, to make bricks by hand and burn them
on the spot in stacks. There are, at least, eight brick
factories at work in the Belfast district. The city, which
is expanding rapidly, is thus supplied, and besides, a
small export trade, which in 1910 amounted to 2000 tons,
is carried on.

Bricks are also made from Glacial clays at Lisburn
and Bangor. Other places in Ulster engaged in
this industry are Dungannon, Porthall near Strabane,
Irvinestown, and Moy near Bundoran. Sand-lime bricks
are made at Newry, and this is the only factory of
its kind in Ireland. The sand used is dredged from
Carlingford Lough.

Peat is the remains of plants in various stages of decay.

Sphagnum and heather are common in high bogs; hypnum, rushes and sedges in morasses. So greatly do mosses enter into the flora of a bog, that the name *moss* is synonymous with *bog* in the North of Ireland and else-where. In decaying, these plants lose a certain amount of their gaseous constituents—Oxygen, Nitrogen and Hydrogen, and have therefore a higher amount of Carbon than their living representatives. Some of the lower bogs cover places originally occupied by lakes, for we find them deeper than the surface of lakes in the vicinity, as at Upper Lough Erne. We also get shell marl as a common basement layer to a bog. Peat grows much more rapidly in the lower than in the higher bogs, but it is difficult to give even approximately the rates of growth. Sphagnum is a moss capable of absorbing from seven to nine times its own weight of water, hence we see a reason for peat being used as litter.

At Maghery, on the southern shore of Lough Neagh, large works have been established for the manufacture of peat litter and peat powder. The Dutch method of cutting the peat is employed here. One feature of this is that the sod is taken off horizontally rather than vertically, as in the older and more usual method of turf-cutting in Ireland. The products are exported to England, and there is also a considerable home trade. These works compare very favourably with others of a similar kind in other parts of the world. It is interesting, too, to find that peat from this factory is used in a gas-producing plant in Portadown.

As regards road metals the material chiefly used in Antrim is basalt. Some of the compact varieties make an excellent stone for this purpose, but basalt often contains cavities filled with minerals which decompose easily and these are a source of weakness to the rock. Great care is therefore required in its selection. Basalt setts from the Giant's Causeway are exported.

In Tyrone, a good road metal is found in a diorite near Cookstown. In Londonderry city a granite sett from Carrigart has been in use for some time. A diorite from Fincarn, north-east of Buncrana, is used for the roads near the city; and for those farther south grits and basalts are employed. In Down, the fine-grained granites from the southern end of the Mourne mountains are exceptionally good. In 1910, 7000 tons of granite, principally setts, were exported from Annalong. In the same year, 9000 tons of setts and blocks were exported from Newry. In the north of Co. Down Silurian grits and basalts are much used for the roads, and at Ballygowan fine-grained dark grits are made into setts, which are much used in Belfast. Setts are also made from basalt at Dundonald. In Donegal, granite and quartzite form good road metal. Limestone, slate and grit, are used in Cavan and Armagh. Some of these grits are of good quality and are almost quartzites. Monaghan has grits with shaly partings as well as coarse diorites and limestones, whilst Fermanagh is supplied with tough, ashy grits, which form good road metal; basaltic rock, calcareous sandstones, and dark limestones are also used.

Building stones are quarried at Dundonald and Scrabo Hill in Triassic sandstone. This is of two colours—red and grey—and both types have been used extensively in the larger buildings in Belfast and elsewhere. In the Lagan valley, similar red sandstones have been used. The old cathedral in Armagh is built of red sandstone, whilst the new cathedral is of limestone. Limestone is used very commonly in Monaghan, Fermanagh, and North Cavan.

Red granite is quarried at Barnesmore, Co. Donegal, and forms a beautiful ornamental stone when polished. A yellow sandstone quarried at Mount Charles, near Donegal, is coming into prominence as a building stone. It has been used in large buildings in Dublin and in the piers of the new bridges over the arms of the Lee in Cork. Granite from the Mourne mountains, and Newry granite, are also used to some extent in building in the neighbouring towns and in Belfast. The dark basalt of Antrim is sometimes roughly squared and dressed, but is more largely used for rubble masonry.

BOTANY

THE province of Ulster, occupying the northern fourth of Ireland, offers a wide variety of surface, and consequently a considerable diversity in its fauna and flora. Large areas in the south and east, especially the counties of Down, Armagh, and Monaghan, are highly tilled, while some other parts, especially the county of Donegal, offer wide stretches of moorland and mountain. The rocks and soils are very varied. Large lakes occur, the most considerable being Lough Neagh and Upper and Lower Lough Erne, which lie in a limestone trough and are studded with islets. In the north-east we have a plateau of Tertiary basalts, forming broad moorlands with precipitous escarpments facing the sea. The coast-line is very varied, and includes several land-locked marine loughs. From the above notes it will be seen that a large variety of conditions is available for plant and animal life.

As compared with the rest of Ireland, the outstanding feature of the Ulster flora is the preponderance of plants which in Great Britain are characteristic of Scotland. These attain their maximum in Antrim, Derry, and Donegal. On the east side of Ireland they are rare south of Down, but on the west they spread in some number down the coast as far as Clare. As examples of " Scottish " plants not found outside Ulster the following may be mentioned :—

Trollius europæus	Pyrola secunda,
Geranium sylvaticum	Melampyrum sylvaticum
Ligusticum scoticum	Equisetrum umbrosum.

Owing to the proximity of Ulster to Scotland, and the general similarity of geological and climatic conditions between the adjoining portions of that country and northern Ireland, this relationship in the flora is to be expected. There can be little doubt that Ireland received much of the northern element in both its fauna and flora by land migration in early times by way of Scotland.

The nature of the flora will be best realised if we take some of the more interesting areas in the province and briefly describe them and their botany.

The Mourne Mountains occupy the southern end of Co. Down, and form a bold and picturesque mass rising in Slieve Donard to 2796 ft. They are composed of granite lapped round by Silurian rocks. The higher hills lie towards the north-east, and here also is situated Tollymore Park, which is good ground for the botanist. Newcastle forms the best centre. The flora of the slate is rather richer than that of the granite. The plants of the district include *Meconopsis cambrica, Saussurea alpina*, many Hieracia including *senescens, hibernicum*, and *argenteum, Cryptogramme crispa*. On the higher grounds *Saxifraga stellaris, Vaccinium Vitis-Idæa, Salix herbacea, Listera cordata, Juniperus nana, Lycopodium alpinum* are characteristic. Several picturesque tarns lie among the hills, and yield *Lobelia Dortmanna* and *Isoetes lacustris*. An interesting hybrid Horsetail, *Equisetum litorale (E. arvense × limosum)* has one of its few Irish stations by the Bann River above Hilltown.

The Silurian area.· One of the largest areas of uniform character to be found in Ulster is the undulating tract occupied by Silurian slates which includes the greater part of Down, Armagh, Monaghan, and Cavan, and only gives way to the prevalent limestone of central Ireland when it reaches the banks of the Shannon. This area is usually hillocky, covered with boulder-clay, and highly tilled; for the botanist interest centres in the lakelets and marshes which occupy the innumerable hollows. In these *Callitriche autumnalis, Cicuta virosa, Polygonum minus, Rumex Hydrolapathum, Typha angustifolia, Sparganium affine, Butomus umbellatus, Potamogeton obtusifolius, Isoetes lacustris*, are characteristic species. The flora is richest in eastern Down, where, perhaps partly on account of a slight admixture of lime in the drift, certain marsh and water plants from the Central Plain creep in. The hydrophile flora of this area includes, in addition to the above-named, *Hottonia palustris, Elatine Hydropiper, Ceratophyllum demersum, Nasturtium sylvestre, Stellaria glauca, Juncus obtusiflorus, Potamogeton plantagineus, Carex teretiuscula, C. filiformis*. The first of these has here its only Irish stations. The second is extremely rare in the British Isles. Most of the rest are abundant Central Plain species, but unknown elsewhere in the north-east.

Lough Neagh. This great lake, the largest in the British Isles, has low shores, generally stony or sandy, with marshes at the mouths of the streams. The level

Spiranthes Romanzoffiana

of the lake was lowered by drainage to the extent of several feet more than half a century ago, since which time some of the characteristic plants have not been seen. Some very interesting species occur. *Spiranthes Romanzoffiana,* a North American orchid, found also in Co. Cork, occurs in marshy meadows in all of the five counties which border the lake, but nowhere else in Europe. The grass *Calamagrostis stricta* var. *Hookeri* is unknown save on the Lough Neagh shores. The sedge *Carex fusca* (=*Buxbaumii*), now possibly extinct on Lough Neagh, occurs elsewhere in the British Isles only by one lake in Scotland. Certain " Highland type " plants, such as *Lobelia Dortmanna* and *Isoetes lacustris*, are frequent. The Lough Neagh flora is also interesting as including a group of maritime plants, rare or unknown in other inland stations in Ireland—*Cerastium semidecandrum, Spergularia rupestris, Viola Curtisii, Erodium cicutarium, Trifolium arvense, Scirpus maritimus, S. Tabernæmontani*. In view of the low level of the lake (48 ft. above sea), some of these may possibly be remnants of a maritime flora existing when a depression of the land allowed the sea to enter the Lough Neagh basin. Some rare marsh plants, such as *Lathyrus palustris*, occur in various places.

The Basaltic Plateau. This area extends over almost the whole of Antrim and much of Derry. On the inland side long heathery and grassy slopes are characteristic, while facing the sea grand glens have been cut deep into the rocks, and marine denudation has produced in places magnificent cliffs. Between the two slopes lie broad moorlands, about 1000 to 1500 ft. in elevation, covered with bog and heather, with shallow lakelets here and there. The nature of the country and its flora may be admirably studied by taking the narrow-gauge railway from Ballymena up the landward slope to Parkmore, situated on the moorland at an elevation of over 1000 feet, and driving thence down the beautiful precipitous vale of Glenariff to the sea at Cushendall. A few rare plants, mostly of Alpine or Scottish type, inhabit the moorlands ; such are *Drosera anglica, Saxifraga Hirculus, Utricularia intermedia, Carex pauciflora,* and *C. irrigua* (the last two not known elsewhere in Ireland). But it is on the basaltic cliffs and deep glens on the seaward side that botanical interest centres, and here a very characteristic flora is developed. On the cliffs and rocky heaths and in the glens we get:

Meconopsis cambrica	Hieracia (many species)
Draba incana	Arctostaphylos Uva-ursi
Arenaria verna	Pyrola media
Sagina subulata	P. minor
Geranium sylvaticum	P. secunda
Vicia sylvatica	Melampyrum sylvaticum
V. Orobus	Orobanche rubra
Dryas octopetala	Taxus baccata
Pyrus Aria	Habenaria albida
Saxifraga hypnoides	Neottia Nidus-avis
S. aizoides	Cryptogramme crispa
Sedum Rhodiola	Equisetum pratense
Epilobium angustifolium	E. trachyodon
Circæa alpina	

and many more interesting species.

Benevenagh and Magilligan. The northern elements in the Ulster flora attains specially well-marked development on the magnificent basaltic precipices of Benevenagh, an isolated hill in Co. Derry lying near the north-western extremity of the basaltic area. The cliff flora there includes:

Draba incana	Hieracia (many species)
Silene acaulis	Salix herbacea
Dryas octopetala	Juniperus nana.
Saxifraga oppositifolia	

Spreading out below the Benevenagh cliffs is the wide sand-flat of Magilligan, which is also excellent ground

u F

for the botanist. *Draba incana* descends from its alpine perch to grow in abundance on the dunes ; *Hypochaeris glabra* has here its only Irish station ; and some other species which are rare locally, such as *Orchis pyramidalis, Epipactis palustris,* and *Lastrea Thelypteris,* may be also found.

Lough Erne. The River Erne, flowing north-westward through a basin of Carboniferous limestone, for forty miles of its course spreads into a great irregular lake-like expansion. A river-like constriction in the middle separates the Upper from the Lower lake. The Upper Lough is a maze of islands, bays and promontories, and the sheltered and marshy nature of its shores is reflected in the flora, which includes *Nasturtium sylvestre, Lathyrus palustris, Cicuta virosa, Stratiotes aloides, Sisyrinchium angustifolium,* and *Carex elongata.* The last but one is perhaps the most interesting, its locality being one of the most northern stations for the " Blue-eyed Grass " of North America, which is so widely spread along the west coast of Ireland. The Lower Lake is more open, with more wood on its many islands. Characteristic plants are *Rhamnus catharticus, Vicia sylvatica, Circæa alpina, Galium boreale, Hieracium umbellatum.* Other noteworthy plants of the Lower Lake are *Caltha radicans* (plentiful about Devenish) and *Potamogeton filiformis* (Kesh).

One of the most interesting areas in Ulster for the botanist lies south-west of Lower Lough Erne, where the tall limestone cliffs of Poulaphuca overlook the lake. This is a hilly area, rising to over 1000 ft., composed partly of limestone, partly of overlying sandstones. The limestone yields among other species *Dryas octopetala, Saxifraga aizoides, S. hypnoides, Circæa alpina,*

Euphrasia Salisburgensis, Sesleria cærulea, Equisetum trachyodon. On the sandstone scarps or in the lakelets of the moorland above are found *Ranunculus scoticus, Meconopsis cambrica, Lobelia Dortmanna, Pyrola secunda, P. media, P. minor, Listera cordata, Trichomanes radicans, Asplenium viride, Equisetum pratense* and many other interesting plants.

Donegal. The County of Donegal presents a wide area of mountain, moor and lake, with deep sea-inlets. It stretches in a north-east and south-west direction for 80 miles, with lower more cultivated land along the south-eastern side. The flora is varied and interesting and tolerably uniform, the most striking change occurring in the extreme south-west, where over a limited area limestone occupies the surface. The effect of this change of rock is to bring in certain plants of the Limestone Plain or of the western limestones, such as *Cornus sanguinea, Gentiana Amarella, Euphrasia Salisburgensis, Juncus obtusiflorus, Sesleria cærulea, Lastrea Thelypteris.* The characteristic flora of the county presents an Alpine and Scottish aspect, and includes among many other uncommon plants—

Thalictrum alpinum	Oxyria digyna
Trollius europæus	Euphorbia hiberna
Crambe maritima	Salix phylicifolia
Draba incana	Eriocaulon septangulare
Silene acaulis	Potamogeton filiformis
Dryas octopetala	Trichomanes radicans
Saxifraga oppositifolia	Adiantum Capillus-Veneris
S. aizoides	Aspidium Lonchitis
S. umbrosa	Equisetum trachyodon
Carum verticillatum	Lycopodium alpinum.
Bartsia viscosa	

While the alpine species descend lower in Donegal than anywhere else in Ireland—pointing apparently to the northern nature of the climate—we are met at the same time by the extremely interesting fact that some of the southern species for which the west of Ireland is famous, which reach in that region a latitude much higher than they attain elsewhere in Europe, mix in Donegal with the alpine flora. Such are *Saxifraga umbrosa*, *Euphorbia hiberna*, *Trichomanes radicans*, *Adiantum Capillus-Veneris*. The occurrence of three of the North American plants of Ireland—namely, *Sisyrinchium angustifolium* (unknown in Europe outside Ireland), *Naias flexilis*, and the Pipewort, *Eriocaulon septangulare* (found also in Skye but not elsewhere in Europe), is also noteworthy. The Donegal flora attains its most pronounced expression on Slieve League, the magnificent cliffs of which, nearly 2000 ft. in height, overlook the waters of Donegal Bay.

The Maritime Flora. The coast-line of Ulster is remarkably varied, and every kind of habitat is represented—lofty cliffs, rocks, great sandy stretches, landlocked bays, muddy estuaries, shingle beaches. The flora is varied similarly. In Down we get the northern limit of some plants which are frequent further south, such as *Trigonella ornithopodioides*, *Artemisia maritima*, *Statice occidentalis*, *Atriplex portulacoides*. Strangford Lough in the same county yields abundance of *Glyceria festucæformis*, a grass elsewhere confined to the Shannon estuary and the Mediterranean. Near Belfast grows the very rare *Zannichellia polycarpa*. The northern Scottish Lovage, *Ligusticum scoticum*, extends along the coast from north Down to north Donegal. The beautiful *Mertensia maritima* is another characteristic

The Irish Spurge (*Euphorbia hiberna*)

northern plant of the Ulster coast. *Zostera nana* is in Ulster found in Down and Donegal. *Scilla verna* is a characteristic plant of the coast of Down, Antrim, and Derry, brightening the short turf in spring with myriads of grey-blue flower-heads.

For mosses Antrim and Down have been well worked, the former particularly. Some of the rare Antrim species extend into Londonderry, where the prevailing rock (basalt) is the same. Donegal also has yielded some very rare mosses, and will doubtless contribute more when it comes to be thoroughly explored.

In the neighbourhood of Belfast we have *Ditrichum vaginans* (whose only known station in the British Isles is on peat on the summit of Colin Hill) ; also the following, which find here their only Irish station :—*Selegeria pusilla* and *S. calcarea* (chalk on Belfast hills) ; *S. Doniana* (Colin Glen) ; *Tortula marginata* (Derriaghy) ; and *Weisia rostellata*. Other mosses which in Ulster are confined to Antrim are *Webera Tozeri* (Derriaghy), *Bryum rubens* (Lisburn), and *B. Mildeanum* (Slemish). Of Co. Down mosses, one of the most interesting is *Catherinea angustata* var. *rhystophylla* (at Saintfield), known elsewhere only from Kent and China. Several other rare species are in Ireland confined to Down— *Fissidens rufulus* and *Hypnum imponens* for example. Other species worthy of mention are *Ditrichum tenuifolium* (Down and Antrim), *D. tortile* (Down, Antrim, Donegal) ; *Campylopus subulatus* (Donegal) ; *Fissidens Curnowii* (Donegal, only Irish station) ; *Grimmia conferta* (Down, Antrim, Derry) ; *G. Doniana* (widespread : in Ireland confined to Ulster) ; *Tortula gracilis* (Down) ; *Barbula Hornschuchiana* (Armagh, Down) ;

Glyceria festucæformis

Weisia calcarea (Down) ; the rare northern *W. fragile*
(Donegal) ; *Ulota calvescens* (Antrim and Donegal, also a
very rare species) ; *Oedipodium Griffithianum* (Donegal) ;
the northern *Tayloria tenuis* (Ben Bradagh, Co. Derry,
only Irish station) ; *Catoscopium nigritum* (Magilligan
sandhills, Co. Derry ; only Irish station) ; the very
rare *Mnium riparium* (Armagh and Antrim) ; *Amblystegium Sprucei* (Fermanagh, only Irish record, also a
rarity); *Hypnum lycopodioides* (Down and Antrim) ;
and *Hylocomium rugosum* (Derry, only Irish station).
Recent additions to the flora include *Dicranum asperulum*
(Cuilcagh, Co. Cavan, only Irish station) ; *Philonotis
seriata* (Monaghan and Armagh) ; *P. adpressa* (Antrim
and Down) ; and *Amblystegium Kochii* (Kilrea, Co.
Derry, only Irish station).

Ulster cannot boast the extraordinary richness in
Scale-mosses which characterises certain districts in
the south and west of Ireland, but nevertheless the flora
is varied, and some very rare plants occur. Several
species find in the province their only Irish stations—
Madotheca rivularis (Monaghan and Down), *Scapania
rosacea* (Slieve League, Co. Donegal), *Metzgeria pubescens*
(Antrim), *Fossombronia cæspitiformis* (Buncrana, Co.
Donegal), *Gymnomitrium obtusum* (Mourne Mountains),
Sphærocarpus Michelii (Colin Glen near Belfast, not
seen recently), *Riccia crystallina* (Co. Antrim). These
are almost all rare plants in Great Britain. The rare
Moerckia hibernica has its only known stations on sand-
dunes in Antrim, Down, and Dublin. Among other
rare species which occur may be mentioned *Radula
Carringtonii* (Lough Erne), *R. voluta* (Cavan), *Cephalo-
ziella stellulifera* (Down), *Gymnomitrium obtusum* (Down),

Diplophyllum obtusifolium (Armagh), *Plagiochila tridenti-
culata* (Donegal and Antrim), *Aplozia cordifolia* (Antrim
and Sperrin Mountains), *Marsupella Funckii* (Antrim,
Down and Armagh), *Ptilidium ciliare* (Antrim), *Petalo-
phyllum Ralfsii* (Derry), *Targionia hypophylla* (Antrim)
and *Riccia sorocarpa* (Derry). Recently *Eremonotus
myriocarpus* has been added to the Irish flora from
Bulbein Mount in Donegal.

Space does not permit of reference to the remaining
great groups of plants—the Fungi, Lichens, and Algæ.
A good deal of work has been done at the first group,
but as regards the Lichens our knowledge is still scanty.
The Algae of some of the large lakes, Lough Neagh in
particular, have received a good deal of attention.

ZOOLOGY

THE Belfast district supplied the original examples of
the so-called " Irish Rat," *Mus hibernicus* of Thompson.
This creature, now known to occur in Great Britain as
well as in several parts of Ireland, has been shown to be
a variety of the common Grey Rat (*M. decumanus*). It
is almost black in colour, and has typically a white
breast. The Badger, (*Meles taxus*), Otter (*Lutra vulgaris*)
and Irish Stoat (*Putorius hibernicus*), are of more or
less frequent occurrence. The Pine Marten (*Mustela
martes*), is still occasionally reported. Round the
coasts, the Great Grey Seal (*Halichærus grypus*), is
not uncommon. As in other Irish districts, the Alpine
Hare (*Lepus variabilis*), is frequent, replacing the Brown
Hare (*L. europæus*) of England. The introduced
Squirrel (*Sciurus vulgaris*) is still local.

Ulster offers a large variety of conditions for bird life. While the wooded areas are generally small in extent, they are numerous except in the highlands of Donegal and Antrim. Lakes and marshes abound, the lakes of the south and centre being generally low-lying, with beds of reeds and water-plants, while in Donegal lakes with rocky and heathery shores are very common. Lough Neagh, the largest sheet of water, is very open, while Lough Erne, next in size, is filled with islands which form ideal breeding grounds. Of the many land-locked marine inlets, Strangford Lough contains innumerable islands and reefs, tenanted in the breeding season by vast numbers of Terns, and by many shore-haunting species. Of mountain and moorland there is also abundance, especially in the north and west.

The more interesting resident birds of the woodlands, etc., include the Blackcap, *Silvia atricapilla* (widespread) ; Garden Warbler, *S. hortensis* (Lagan valley and Lough Erne) ; Golden-crested Wren, *Regulus cristatus* (common) ; Tree-Creeper, *Certhia familiaris* (widespread) ; Siskin, *Carduelis spinus* (common) ; Long-eared Owl, *Asio otus* (frequent) ; Stock-Dove, *Columba œnas* (a recent arrival in Ireland, increasing) ; Heron, *Ardea cinerea* (frequent) ; Crossbill, *Loxia curvirostra* (local) : the Tree-Sparrow *Passer montanus*, has been recently observed at Portrush and in three places in Donegal ; it is very local in Ireland.

On the rivers, the Kingfisher, *Alcedo ispida*, is characteristic of the lower reaches, and the Irish form of the Dipper, *Cinclus aquaticus*, of the upper reaches among the hills. The Grey Wagtail, *Motacilla melanope* is also a familiar sight.

The lacustrine avifauna of Ulster is important, as the

large lakes, such as Lough Erne and Lough Neagh, have an abundant bird population. Among the breeding species are the Tufted Duck, *Fuligula cristata* (now widespread), Shoveller, *Spatula clypeata* (increasing) ; Common Scoter, *Oedemia nigra* (recently found breeding on Lough Erne) ; Red-breasted Merganser, *Mergus serrator* (frequent ; also on marine islands) ; several species of Gulls and Terns ; Oyster-catcher, *Hæmatopus ostralegus* (breeding on Lough Neagh) ; Great Crested Grebe, *Podicipes cristatus* (frequent) ; and Red-throated Diver, *Colymbus septentrionalis* (one breeding station). The Yellow Wagtail, *Motacilla Raii*, breeds in Ireland only about Lough Neagh in Ulster, and Loughs Corrib, Mask, and Carra in Connaught.

On heaths and bogs we find nesting numbers of Wheatears, *Saxicola œnanthe*, and Stonechats, *Pratincola rubicola* ; also the Merlin, *Falco æsolon*, Curlew, *Numenius arquata*, and so on ; while the mountains are the home of the Ring Ouzel, *Turdus torquatus* ; Raven, *Corvus corax ;* Peregrine, *Falco peregrinus ;* and Golden Plover, *Charadrius pluvialis ;* all of which are widespread, though not abundant.

As regards the shore-breeding birds, the low coasts of Co. Down, and especially the numerous gravelly islets of the land-locked inlet of Strangford Lough afford suitable nesting-sites for an abundant avifauna—-Arctic Terns, *Sterna macrura* ; Common Terns, *S. fluviatilis* ; Little Terns, *S. minuta* ; Ringed Plover, *Ægialitis hiaticola* ; Oyster-catchers, *Hæmatopus ostralegus* ; Sheld-duck, *Tadorna cornuta* ; and Red-breasted Mergansers, *Mergus serrator*. Most of these species are found again on Mew Island off Donaghadee, which is another great Tern colony ; here the Roseate Tern,

Sterna Dougalli, bred until about 40 years ago. The Sandwich Tern, *S. cantiaca* has been found breeding in Down, Fermanagh, and Donegal. The only other Irish colony at present known is in Mayo. The lofty cliffs of Rathlin Island, and of some of the Donegal promontories, such as Horn Head, support vast colonies of breeding sea-birds, mainly Guillemots, *Uria troile* ; Razorbills, *Alca torda* ; Puffins, *Fratercula arctica* ; Shags, *Phalacrocorax graculus* ; Kittiwakes, *Rissa tridactyla* ; Herring Gulls, *Larus argentatus* ; and Lesser Black-backed Gulls, *L. fuscus*. The less common breeders on the sea-cliffs and shores include the Manx Shearwater, *Puffinus anglorum* ; Storm-Petrel, *Procellaria pelagica* ; Chough, *Pyrrhocorax graculus* ; Peregrine, *Falco peregrinus* ; and Raven, *Corvus corax*. The latest addition to the fauna is the Fulmar, *Fulmarus glacialis*, which has taken up residence during the breeding season in two places.

In winter, the land-birds are reinforced by great numbers of immigrants, such as Fieldfares, *Turdus pilaris* ; Redwings, *T. iliacus* ; and Sky-larks, *Alauda arvensis* ; while the aquatic fauna, both fresh-water and marine, includes vast numbers of Ducks and Geese from the north. Among the rarer winter visitors are the Great Spotted Woodpecker, *Dendrocopus major* ; Great Grey Shrike, *Lanius excubitor* ; Snowy Owl, *Nyctea scandiaca* ; Greenland Falcon, *Falco candicans* ; and King Eider, *Somateria spectabilis*. The Glaucous and Iceland Gulls, *Larus glaucus* and *L. leucopterus*, are occasionally seen.

Among the breeding birds which have increased in the district are the Mistle-Thrush, *Turdus viscivorus*, now breeding everywhere, of which the first known

Irish example was shot in Co. Antrim in 1808 ; Bullfinch, *Pyrrhula europæa* ; Grasshopper Warbler, *Locustella nævia* ; Starling, *Sturnus vulgaris* (quite rare half a century ago ; now everywhere) ; Magpie, *Pica rustica* (first seen in Ireland about 1680) ; Jackdaw, *Corvus monedula* ; Tufted Duck, *Fuligula cristata* (first found breeding in Ireland about thirty-five years ago, on Lough Erne) ; Stock-Dove, *Columba œnas* (discovered breeding about the same date as the last, in Co. Down) ; and Woodcock, *Scolopax rusticula* (now breeds in every county). The birds which have now ceased to breed in Ulster include the Golden Eagle, *Aquila chrysaëtus* (once on most of the mountain-ranges, now extinct) ; Buzzard, *Buteo vulgaris* ; White-tailed Eagle, *Haliaëtus albicilla* ; and Marsh Harrier, *Circus æruginosus* (all formerly widespread). The Hen Harrier, *Circus cyaneus*, appears to be on the verge of extinction. The Quail, *Coturnix communis*, formerly abundant, is now rare.

Belfast has been, like Dublin, long a centre for ornithological study, and in its vicinity and the neighbouring counties, a number of rare stragglers have been shot and identified. Among these are the only Irish-taken examples of the Two-barred Crossbill, *Loxia bifasciata*, (Antrim and Fermanagh) ; Purple Heron, *Ardea purpurea* (Co. Monaghan) ; Broad-billed Sandpiper, *Limicola platyrhyncha* (Belfast Lough) ; Bonaparte's Gull, *Larus philadelphia* (Belfast) ; and Wilson's Petrel, *Oceanites oceanicus* (Lough Erne and Co. Down.)

The Vivaparous Lizard (*Lacerta vivipara*), the only Irish reptile, is frequent, as are also the Common Frog (*Rana temporaria*), and the Common Newt (*Molge vulgaris*). The only other Irish amphibian, the

Natterjack Toad (*Bufo calamita*), is confined to a small area at the extreme opposite end of the country, in Co. Kerry.

The Salmon, *Salmo salar*, is common, and many important fisheries exist. The Brown Trout, *S. fario* is everywhere ; var. *estuarius* is frequent ; var. *ferox* and *stomachicus* are frequent in Lough Neagh, where the former has been taken up to 36 lbs. weight. The endemic Pollan, *Coregonus pollan*, occurs in numbers in

The Pollan

Lough Neagh. The Lough Neagh Pollan fishery is very important, being valued at £6000 to £7000 annually, and giving employment to about 500 men. The distribution of the Pollan group shows a similarity to that of the endemic shrimp *Mysis relicta*, which forms part of its food. The Pollan which occurs in Lough Erne is now considered to be a distinct species, *C. altior*. A curious point in local ichthyology is that the Charr, *Salvelinus sp.* used also to be common in Lough Neagh, but disappeared early in the nineteenth century. The more frequent form of this variable fish, *S. Colei*, has been taken in Loughs Eask and Derg in Donegal, and *S. Grayi* in Lough

Melvin, Fermanagh. Another form recently described as *S. Trevelyani*, occurs only in Lough Finn, Co. Donegal. The Sea Trout, *S. trutta*, is common, both in its typical form and in its variety *S. cambricus*. The two Shads, *Clupea finta* and *C. alosa*, occur occasionally.

The molluscan fauna of Ulster is large and varied, the result of the diversified nature of the surface. In many of the coastal regions, such as the shores of Antrim and Donegal, the combination of cliffs, sand-dunes, and glens filled with native scrub, results in a large molluscan population. For instance, the Ballycastle district in Antrim has a remarkably rich fauna, including *Vertigo alpestris* and *V. angustior*, *Helicella barbara*, and *Arianta arbustorum*, which is very local in Ireland. The great expanse of Lough Neagh does not present any special features ; but it has recently yielded *Succinea oblonga* (near Antrim Castle), and also the first recorded inland locality in Ireland for *Paludestrina Jenkinsi*. The Lough Erne basin is richer, yielding among other species *Limnæa prætenuis* (in lakelets off the limestone), an endemic form found elsewhere only in Kerry ; *Pisidium Lilljeborgi*, *Arianta arbustorum*, and *Clausilia laminata*, all of which are rare and local in Ireland. At the mouth of the River Erne, the Bundoran sand-hills are famous for the extraordinary number of reversed *Helix nemoralis* which they have yielded.

The most characteristically Ulster mollusk is the rare *Vertigo alpestris*, which in Ireland is known only from three Ulster stations, all near sea-level—Coleraine, Whitepark Bay, and Port Salon. Other interesting species which occur are *Zonitoides excavatus* (north-west), *Helicella barbara* (whole coast), *Acanthinula lamellata*

(widespread), *Cæcilioides acicula* (Monaghan and Cavan),
Pupa anglica (everywhere), *Vertigo pusilla* (north, mostly
dead), *Succinea oblonga* (Antrim, Fermanagh, E. Donegal),
Acicula lineata (widespread), *Margaritana margaritifera*
(widespread), *Pisidium Lilljeborgi* (Fermanagh, Antrim,
and W. Donegal). The absence from the whole west
and north-west of *Helicella virgata*, a species otherwise
very widespread in Ireland, is remarkable.

In Ulster, Lepidoptera have been more widely, if not
more intensively, collected than in many other parts of
Ireland, and there are some rare insects reported from
almost every county. A few species have not been
captured in any other part of Ireland—*Nudaria senex*,
Agrotis puta, and *Tethia subtusa* (all from Enniskillen),
and the rare *Heliothis scutosa* (Buncrana, Co. Donegal).
The ab. *gaëlica* of *Cymatophora or* has been described by
Kane from a single example captured at Farnham, Co.
Cavan. The rarer species found in the province also
include *Colias edusa* (Monaghan and Armagh) ; *Gonep-
teryx rhamni* (a local species in Ireland, very rare in
Ulster) ; *Leucophasia sinapis* (Enniskillen) ; *Lycæna
ægon* (Rostrevor) ; *Deilephila livornica* (two taken in
Ormeau Park, Belfast) ; *Sphinx convolvuli* (Glenarm).
Of the Burnet Moths, *Z. trifolii* occurs in four counties,
but *Z. lonicerae* has been taken only near Armagh.
Drepana falcula has been taken at Favour Royal (Tyrone)
and Enniskillen ; *Trichiura cratægi* at Magilligan ;
Dicranura bifida near Londonderry ; and larvæ of the
Lobster Moth, *Stauropus fagi* have been obtained at
Belleisle on Lough Erne. Among the Noctuids may be
mentioned *Mamesta albicolon* (one at Magilligan) ;
Cerastis ligula (Tyrone, Cavan, and Antrim) ; *Aplecta*

occulta (one near Londonderry) ; *Hadena trifolii* (Kilderry, Co. Donegal) ; and *Dasypolia templi* (Glenarm). The rarer geometers include *Nyssia zonaria* (abundant on sandhills at Ballycastle) ; *Dasydia obfuscaria* (coast at Narin, Donegal) ; *Hybernia aurantiaria* (Favour Royal) ; *Chematobia borealis* (Drumreaske, Monaghan) ; *Oporabia autumnaria* (hills near Belfast) ; the northern *Larentia flavicinctata* (Murlough Bay, Antrim, on *Saxifraga hypnoides*) ; *Emmelesia decolorata, E. minorata* and *E. valerianata* (the first here and there on the east coast, the second in the Mourne mountains, and the last at Farnham in Cavan) ; *Phibalapteryx lapidata* (Antrim and Donegal mountains) ; and *Mesotype virgata* (Newcastle, Co. Down).

The most interesting feature of the beetle fauna of Ulster is the occurrence around the shores of Lough Neagh of several extremely rare species. Three species which occur there are unknown elsewhere in the British Isles— the rare *Dyschirius obscurus* (S. and N.E. shores, preying on *Bledius subterraneus*), the northern *Bembidium argenteolum* (Ardmore and Shane's Castle), and *Cryptophagus bimaculatus* (frequent in reed beds at Shane's Castle). *Stenus palposus*, unknown in Great Britain, has its only Irish stations at Lough Neagh and in Meath. Other rare Lough Neagh beetles are *Silpha dispar, Hæmonia appendiculata*, and *Ceuthorrhynchus arcuatus*. The Ulster fauna includes a good many species which are northern in their range in Great Britain and on the Continent, such as *Blethisa multipunctata* (common), *Silpha quadripunctata* (Rostrevor), *Lema septentrionalis* (frequent), *Otiorrhynchus blandus* (frequent), and *Erirrhinus æthiops* (local). Among the species which in

u G

Ireland are unknown outside the province are *Harpalus neglectus* (Rathlin Island), the two conspicuous water-beetles—*Dytiscus circumcinctus* (Armagh) and *D. lap-*

Pelophila borealis, and its distribution in the British Isles

ponicus (mountain tarns in Donegal), *Quedius obliteratus* (Co. Cavan), *Philonthus lucens* (frequent on lake shores), *Xantholinus cribripennis* (sandhills in Donegal and Derry), *Epuræa angustula* (Donegal), and *Cleonus sulcirostris* (Down). On mountains and bogs we get *Carabus glabratus*, *C. clathratus*, *C. nitens* (each in several counties), *Leistus montanus* (Mourne mountains), and *Cymindis vaporariorum* (Donegal). Rock-pools on the coast yield *Octhebius Lejolisi*, and salt-marshes *Telephorus darwinianus*. The rare *Pelophila borealis* is recorded from lake shores in six counties. The Pyrenean weevil *Otiorrhynchus auropunctatus*, unknown in Great Britain, ranges along the east coast of Ireland into our district, having been taken near Londonderry. Another rarity, though familiar in Ireland, is *Rhopalomesites Tardyi*, which is widespread in Ulster. Among other species may be mentioned *Bembidium quadriguttatum* (near Belfast), *Lebia chlorocephala* (Lough Swilly), *Pselphus dresdensis* (Armagh), the endemic *Silpha subrotundata* (common), the Musk Beetle, *Aromia moschata* (near Belfast), and *Pterostichus aterrimus* (Cavan).

Among the most interesting spiders of Ulster are two species of Erigone taken a few years ago by Mr Welch of Belfast—namely *E. Welchii* found near Bunbeg in Donegal, and unknown elsewhere, and *E. capra*, taken on the canal bank close to Monaghan and known elsewhere only from one station in France. Four species which are confined to the British Isles have been found within the province—*Tmeticus simplex* (Down, only Irish station), *Theonoe minutissima* (Donegal, also in Connaught), *Styloctetor uncinus* (Down, also in Munster), and *Microneta decora* (Antrim, also in West Leinster). The rarer Irish species found only in Ulster also include : *Philodromus emarginatus* and *Pedanostethus neglectus* (Fermanagh) ; the northern *Dicymbium tibiale* (Donegal); *Walckenæra nodosa* (Monaghan) ; *Lophocarenum Mengei* (Monaghan, Fermanagh, Armagh) ; *Tmeticus expertus* and *T. rufus* (Armagh). The rarer Ulster species which are also found elsewhere in Ireland, include *Euophrys petrensis* (Antrim) ; *Cnephalocotes obscurus* and *C. interjectus* (Down) ; *Diplocephalus Beckii* (Antrim) ; *D. castiniepes* (Donegal) ; *Hilaira excisa* (Fermanagh and Antrim ;) *H. uncata* (Monaghan and Armagh) ; *Bathyphantes parvulus* (Down and Antrim) ; *Porrhomma Thorellii* (Fermanagh and Antrim) ; and *Attus floricola* (Fermanagh).

Having dealt above with some of the larger and

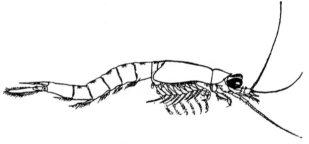

Mysis relicta

better known groups of Invertebrates, space permits of only a reference to a few additional creatures, interesting on account of their distribution. The only specimens of the hymenopteron *Lissanota basalis* as yet taken in the British Isles were recently obtained in Co. Down. Among the dragonflies, *Ischnura pumilio* and *Erythromma najas* occur, both having been taken in the Belfast district ; these are very local insects in Great Britain. The large water-bug *Aphelochirus æstivalis* is found in Lough Neagh, where also the rare shrimp *Mysis relicta* occurs in vast numbers—a species absent

from Great Britain, though ranging across northern
Europe and America. The interesting Purple Sea-
urchin, *Strongylocentrotus lividus*, abundant on the
western coast of Ireland, extends northwards into
Donegal. The fresh-water sponge *Heteromeyenia Ryderi*
has been found in lakes in several Ulster counties ; it is
a typical North American species, elsewhere known only
from Ireland and Scotland.

ANTIQUITIES

THE province of Ulster provides important material for
the study of Irish Stone-Age antiquities. The space
at the writer's command precludes more than a sketch
of these, but a few of the sites, where worked flints
etc. have been found, are described.

As well as Stone-Age antiquities, Ulster has produced
some finds of associated objects of unusual interest and
value, including the gold ornaments found at Broighter ;
and the important crannog finds, of Iron-Age date, from
Lisnacroghera, Co. Antrim.

The province has proved rich in Bronze-Age antiquities, and it would seem that from early Neolithic
times, Ulster has been inhabited by a thriving population.
In the Irish Heroic period (which corresponds with
the La Tène, or second Iron-Age), Ulster, as portrayed
by the Irish Sagas, played a prominent part. The
relations, hostile or friendly, between Ulster and Connaught, lie at the base of the prose epics belonging to the
Cuchulainn cycle. The heroes of Ulster are portrayed

to us as grouped together at *Eamhain Mhacha* (Armagh), under the leadership of King Conchobhar Mac Neasa (Connor Mac Nessa), in the House of the Red Branch, (*Craobh Ruadh*).   Their assembly has been compared to the fellowship of the Knights of the Round Table under Britain's hero, King Arthur.

As mentioned in the *Ireland* volume in this series,

Typical Flint-flakes from the River Bann

the north-east of the country has been the centre for research into the history of Neolithic man in Ireland, being the only part in which flint is found *in situ.*   Chalk with bands of flints is a characteristic feature of the scenery of Antrim and Londonderry, flint having been plentifully strewn over these and the adjoining counties, by the ice streams of the Glacial period.   The most important remains of the settlements of Stone-Age man are the raised beaches at Larne, Whitepark Bay, Island Magee, Portrush, Portstewart, etc. As well as at these settlements, flint flakes and implements have been found nearly everywhere along the shores of the River Bann ; several stations having produced implements and flakes in profusion. Many implements and flakes have been found at Mount Sandal, south of Coleraine, and at Kilrea : implements have also been found at Portglenone, Gortgole, Culbane, and at other places as far as Toome Bar where the Bann leaves Lough Neagh.

Larne, a long, tapering gravel-spit rising from some 10 to 20 ft. above high-water mark, extending from the west side of the narrow entrance of Larne Lough into the waters of the bay for about three-quarters of a mile, is the principal raised beach site. The gravels contain numerous marine shells and worked flakes are found with these. Since Mr G. V. Du Noyer of the Geological Survey first called attention to the site in 1868, numerous collectors have resorted to it for the purpose of gathering the flakes, which lie about in such abundance that strangers to the district are led to doubt their human workmanship. The Belfast Naturalists Field Club appointed a committee in 1886 to investigate the Larne gravels, and the final report of this committee was drawn up in 1889. In 1897 Messrs George Coffey and R. Lloyd Praeger made a scientific examination of the Larne gravels, and on this occasion a series of typical implements and a section of the gravels were obtained and deposited in the National Museum, Dublin.

The chief fact of importance established by this examination was that the whole movement of depression took place during Neolithic times, and that man was living on the ground during the submergence. The Neolithic date of the raised beaches and consequently of the implements found therein was thus established.

The most typical implements of human workmanship found at Larne are flakes, which are strewn on the beach in large numbers. The flakes on the surface layers are white while those at the lower levels are cream coloured ; they have been so greatly rolled that their edges are much abraded, but the bulb of percussion can generally be seen. The large majority of these flakes appear to be wasters struck off the outer surface of the flint nodule in order to reduce it to the proper truncated-cone shape from which useful flakes could be obtained. As well as flakes, numerous flint cores have been found, also the typical implements known as the " Larne " celts. The " Larne " celts are more or less pointed implements without a cutting edge, resembling those from Cissbury near Worthing, Sussex. Mr Coffey, in his report of the examination of 1897 referred to above, came to the conclusion that Larne was not a dwelling-site, but a place of manufacture where flint was sought and flaked to carry away, this being the explanation of the enormous number of flint flakes and waste cores to be there found, the Larne celt being merely a roughed-out implement intended to be removed and finished off elsewhere. On the other hand, some authorities consider the Larne " celt " to have been a finished implement in the form of a pick, and the industry of Larne to belong to the same cultural level as the well-known station of Campigny in France.

Many sites occupied by Neolithic man are to be found in the sandhills of the north coast of Ireland. These sandhills lie above the raised beaches, and, when the

wind lays bare old surfaces among the hollows, pottery
and worked flints are found.   The best known of these
are at Whitepark Bay, Co. Antrim ; Dundrum Bay,

Neolithic Stone Axe-heads from the North of Ireland

Co. Down ; and the mouth of the River Bann, near
Portstewart, Co. Londonderry.   Among the flints found
are numerous cores and flakes, while scrapers of various
sizes, some being exceedingly small, are also discovered
in large numbers, showing that the working of flint was

carried on extensively in the sandhills. Polished axes have also been found at these sites, while highly finished arrowheads and hollow scrapers have been discovered at Dundrum Bay and Portstewart. The pottery obtained from these settlements is often decorated with incised lines, etc., and judging from some of the objects discovered, it is probable that the human occupation of the sites lasted from Neolithic times into the early Iron Age and the Christian period.

The flakes obtained from sites on the River Bann are often carefully flaked and trimmed. The typical flake is leaf-shaped with a well-marked bulb of percussion, it has generally a brownish patina. The implements from the Bann, include axe-heads of the kitchen-midden type, scrapers, pointed implements, and a few ordinary polished celts.

The axe factories discovered by Mr W. J. Knowles in the neighbourhood of Cushendall are interesting remains of the Neolithic period in Co. Antrim. On one of these sites situated in a field in Glen Ballyemon, were found numerous pieces of natural rock partly chipped, many rough axes, flakes, and hammer stones. The flakes appeared to have been struck off the boulders when making axes, some were dressed into spear-points and scrapers. The rock from which the axes, etc., were manufactured is a kind of altered fine-grained diorite. No traces of kitchen middens were found ; and the site does not appear to have been a dwelling-place, but a ground where the implements were made. Another similar site was discovered at Clougheen and at Tievebulliagh, the latter place was very rich in objects, a great many axes and thousands of flakes being discovered. Many of the flakes were worked into forms

recalling French palæolithic scrapers. In no cases were
any traces of human habitation discovered, so it is to
be assumed that the sites were merely used for manu-
facturing the implements in the rough, and that they
were taken elsewhere to be finished.

There are, according to a computation in Borlase's
Dolmens of Ireland (1897), two hundred and twenty-
seven dolmens in Ulster, Donegal heading the list of
counties with no less than eighty-two. One of these,
that of Annacloghmullin, Co. Armagh, has been entirely
destroyed in recent times ; it is probable that others
have shared the same fate. The dolmen in the Giant's
Ring near Belfast will be described in the account of the
earthwork which surrounds it. As typical of the dolmens of Co. Down the structure known as the Sliddery-
ford dolmen at Newcastle may be mentioned. It is
situated in a field close to the road from Dundrum to
Newcastle, within 1½ miles of Dundrum. The dolmen
stands about 9 ft. high, and the granite cap-stone, which
measures 8 ft. by 7½ ft., is 3½ ft. thick. A little distance
from the dolmen is a large pillar stone measuring 11 ft.
3 in. in height from the ground. Another well-known
Co. Down dolmen is that of Legananny, which stands
on the western slope of Boley Lough about 6 miles north-
west of Castlewellan in the townland of Legananny.
The cap-stone is a coffin-shaped granite slab, measuring
11 ft. in length and 5 ft. in width at the broadest part ;
it is supported by 3 pillars. The Kempe Stone dolmen
in the same county also deserves mention ; it is not far
from the village of Dundonald. The cap-stone is of large
dimensions and covers a chamber formed of six large
blocks. Human bones were discovered in 1830 on

excavating the chamber, in which in 1897 Mr Hugh Kirk of Newtownards discovered the fragment of a decorated food vessel of Bronze-Age date.

Many of the dolmens are in a ruined condition. The largest of the two monuments at Kilcloony deserves description. The cap-stone measures 20 ft. long by

Kempe Stone Dolmen, Co. Down

13 ft. broad, and is in places 3 ft. thick. It is supported by two pillars at the east end, each about 6 ft. in height, and slopes to the west, resting on a low slab which forms the end of the chamber. A smaller dolmen of similar construction lies some yards to the west of this. There is also a remarkable series of monuments in the townland of Finner, parish of Inishmacsaint, consisting of several dolmens, and a carn containing a dolmen-like chamber ; the carn has been ruined, and

burnt human bones were discovered in the cist. A short distance from the carn were discovered a grave containing burnt bones, and an urn ; close by are traces of two stone circles. The destruction of the dolmen of Annacloghmullin, Co. Armagh, alluded to above, is to be deplored, for this dolmen, according to Borlase's illustration of it, corresponded by its semicircular front and method of roofing to the structures known as the " Tombs of the Giants " in Sardinia. Consequently it was of importance for the comparative study of pre-historic monuments.

The remains of the tumulus and rude stone grave at Knockmany, Co. Tyrone, is situated on a hill overlooking the River Blackwater. The tomb of Knockmany is traditionally associated with the burial place of Baine, who died in A.D. III, but the grave is considerably earlier than this. The tomb resembles a dolmen in form ; the stones of which it is composed are of red sandstone, or mill-stone grit. The monument was originally covered by a carn, now quite destroyed. The chamber was placed at the margin of the carn, the arrangement recalling that of an ordinary passage tomb. An interesting feature of the monument is the scribings to be found on some of the stones which compose the chamber. One of these markings is a human face, others take the form of cups and rings, while a few are of a curious zig-zag shape. Some have supposed that the decoration is ornamental in character ; but it probably contained some symbolical meaning.

The stone circle of Ballynoe about 3 miles from Down-patrick is a remarkable monument. It is a complete

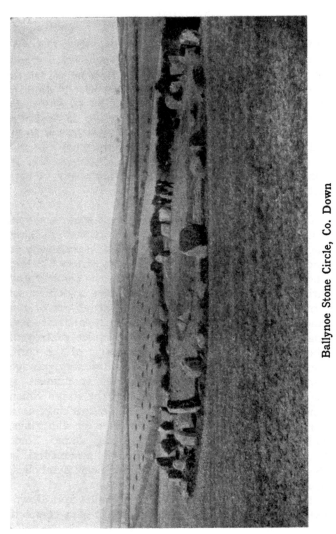

Ballynoe Stone Circle, Co. Down

circle of large stones, mostly of Ordovician grit, with a
diameter of about 100 ft.   Inside this is an ellipse of
smaller stones about 90 ft. by 40 ft.   The largest of the
stones in the outer ring stands about 6½ ft. in height.

The most interesting "find" discovered in this province,
is also one of the best known Irish finds, as it became
the subject of an important law-suit on the question of
treasure trove ; it was unearthed in 1896 at Broighter,
Limavady, Co. Londonderry.   The antiquities found,
consisted of a model of a boat in gold, with mast, oars,
grappling iron, and three forked implements ; a bowl,
two chains, a collar, a twisted necklet, and portion of
another, all of gold.   They were discovered when
ploughing a field on a farm in the townland of Broighter,
and were purchased by the late Mr Robert Day, of Cork,
who sold them to the British Museum.   A lawsuit was
subsequently instituted on behalf of the Irish National
Collection on the grounds that the objects were treasure
trove and belonged to the Crown, who had vested the
right of treasure trove over objects found in Ireland
in the Royal Irish Academy.   Judgment was finally
given in favour of the Crown ;   the objects were
returned to Ireland, and are now exhibited in the
National Museum, Dublin.   The gold collar is one of
the finest specimens of a Late-Celtic collar known ; it
was made of two plates of gold, folded over and soldered
together ; its decoration consists of repoussé work in
the form of trumpet-pattern, the background between
the spaces of the raised pattern being filled in with
finely-engraved concentric lines executed with a compass.
It was fastened on the neck by means of a projecting
stud, fitting into a slot at the end of the opposite side ;

the collar is capable of being turned at right angles for the purpose of opening or closing this. The boat measures 7¼ ins. in length and 3 ins. in breadth, and contained nine seats. It is made of a sheet of gold plate, divided and rejoined at the prow and stem. The central seat is pierced for the insertion of the mast ; the rowlocks are formed of wire rings. The bowl measures 3½ ins. in diameter and is about 2 ins. in height ; it is beaten out of a thin plate of gold ; it weighs 1 oz. 4 dwts. 12 grs. It has four small rings let into the rim at equal distances for suspension. The chains are of exquisite fineness and workmanship, resembling those attached to the Tara Brooch and to the pin found at Clonmacnois. The antiquities may probably be dated to the first century B.C.

Interesting relics of the Scandinavian raids on this province are a pair of Norse brooches and a bronze bowl found in 1903 in a hillock on a portion of the raised beach of Ballyholme between Bangor and Groomsport, Co. Down. The brooches belong to the early part of the ninth century, and as the *Irish Annals* record a raid by Northern vikings on Bangor Abbey in A.D. 824, probably a Norse woman was buried on the spot where the brooches were found. This interesting find is preserved in the National Museum, Dublin ; in the same collection is another somewhat later Scandinavian brooch found near the River Bann. Scandinavian coins are also stated to have been discovered in various parts of Ulster.

The principal earthwork of the province, and one of the most important in Ireland is the great fort which lies about 1½ miles to the west of the city of Armagh.

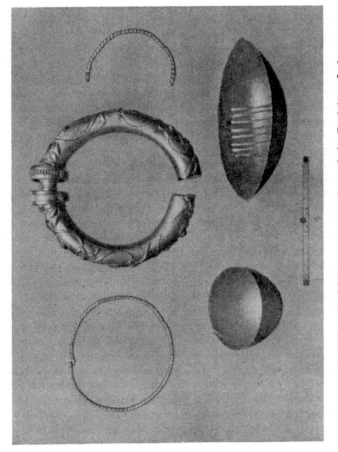

Gold Collar, Model Boat. etc., portions of the Broighter find

It is generally known as the " Navan fort," but its Irish name is *Eamhain Mhacha*. It was the royal residence of the kings of Ulster, and its foundation dates from about 300 B.C. The legendary account of its origin is as follows: Three kings of Ulster, Aodh Ruadh, Diothorba and Ciombaoth agreed to reign in alternate succession for seven years. Having each enjoyed possession for the agreed on term three times, Aodh Ruadh died, and his daughter Macha claimed her father's turn of the sovereignty. She was opposed by Diothorba and Ciombaoth but she defeated them, Diothorba being slain. The five sons of Diothorba demanded the sovereignty after Macha had reigned seven years, but she refused to resign, and defeated them in battle, after which they were compelled to build her a rath, the plan of which she traced out with her golden brooch. Hence the place was called *Eomhuin* from *eó*, a brooch and *muin* the neck. Macha married Ciombaoth, so that all the claimants were disposed of. The Knights of the Red Branch, a band of heroes, recalling the Knights of the Round Table, were named from one of the houses of the palace of *Eamhain* called the *Craobh Ruadh*, or the Red Branch, where they received their military training. The palace, as such, was destroyed, tradition says, about A.D. 332, after having been the chief royal residence of Ulster for over six hundred years. The remains consist of a great earthwork which forms an irregular circle about 850 ft. across. On the side nearest to Armagh the earthwork has been almost entirely " improved " away, but, on the western side, the wall and fosse are fairly complete. At the highest portion of the enclosure there is a large mound which has the appearance of a tumulus, and may be the place

where Queen Macha was buried. Some distance from
this is a ring-fort which possibly represents the palace

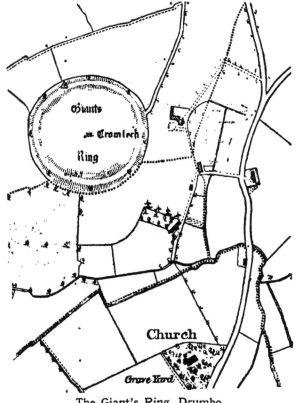

The Giant's Ring, Drumbo

site. he whole enclosure contains about 11 acres.
The earthwork next in importance to *Eamhain Mhacha*

is the fort of Downpatrick. This great construction lies about a quarter of a mile north of Downpatrick Cathedral. According to tradition it was, in the first century, the residence of one of the Red Branch Knights called Ceileachair. The earthwork measures about 2100 ft. in circumference, while the mound measures 60 ft. in height ; it is encircled by three ramparts 30 ft. wide. It has been argued that the fort of Downpatrick is really a mote of Norman origin, and that the traditional name, *Raith Ceileachair*, has been wrongly applied to it, being really the name of the rath within which the ancient monastery at Downpatrick was entrenched. If this view be correct, the great fort was probably the *castrum* erected by John de Courcy in 1177.[1]

Another earthwork of interest is the so-called " Giant's Ring," at Drumbo, about half-an-hour's drive from the city of Belfast. This enormous earthen ring is about 580 ft. in diameter, its rampart varies from 10 to 20 ft. in height, and is 80 ft. thick at the base. There are at present seven openings in the circle, possibly representing the original entrances to the enclosure. In the centre of the fort is a dolmen consisting of seven stones on end, supporting a cover-stone. It is difficult to date an earthwork of this type, but, from the presence inside it of the dolmen, it may be inferred that its use was sepulchral and ceremonial rather than defensive. Recent excavation has failed to find any traces of a burial beneath the dolmen. Probably the site was looted in ancient times.

A large and remarkable earthwork of irregular plan

[1] A recent excavation of the fort (1920) has resulted in the discovery of fragments of pottery, etc., of mediæval date, showing that the occupation of the site continued down to late times.

known as the Dun at Dorsey, is situated in the barony of
Upper Fews, Co. Armagh. It measures about 1 mile
from east to west and it is 600 yards across. The
defences consist of an earthwork with deep fosses on
each side, and lesser mounds on the outside. Two
streams intersect the site, and in the marshy parts the
rampart rested on piles. There are two small knolls
of rock in the centre of the fort, which are defended by
dry stone ring walls, and on the south-west inside the
earthwork is a stone pillar. The date of the erection of
this vast construction is difficult to determine.

An interesting fort in this province is the stone fort
or *cashel* called *Grianán Ailigh* (the summer-house of
Ailech), about 7 miles from Derry in the Co. Donegal.
It is a strong fortress situated on a hill about 800 ft.
high commanding a fine view over Lough Swilly.
It is surrounded by three concentric ramparts, which
are in a much dilapidated state, but appear to have
been made of earth mixed with stone. The cashel
itself is built of large uncemented stones of grey schist
averaging about 2 ft. in length and in many cases
roughly squared. The wall which encloses an area of
about 77 ft. in diameter, is some 16 ft. high with an
average width of 13 ft. It had a slight curve inwards
like the Staigue Fort, Co. Kerry; it must originally
have been much higher. There is a terrace about 5 ft.
from the base of the wall, which was reached by flights
of steps placed on each side of the entrance. At one time
there were a succession of terraces ascending to the top
of the wall. This fort was repaired about 1870-75 by
Dr Bernard, who marked in black colour the walls at
the level at which he commenced rebuilding. *Grianán
Ailigh* was an important residence of the local princes

and is mentioned in the *Irish Annals*. It was destroyed and deserted in A.D. 674 ; in 1101 it was demolished by Muircheartach Ó Briain king of Munster, after which date it does not appear to have been rebuilt.

Among the fortifications of this province the so-called bawns erected in the Plantation period may be mentioned. Under the Orders and Conditions of the Plantation, undertakers were required, by the terms of the letters patent granting them their estates, to erect defensive buildings for the protection of the plantation within two years of the date of the grants. The regulations provided that the grantee of 2000 acres should erect a castle with a strong bawn ; for a grant of 1500 acres, a strong house of stone or brick with a strong bawn was required ; while the grantee of 1000 acres must erect a strong bawn. The castle and bawn of Dungiven is an interesting example of these enclosures, it was built by Captain Edward Dodington, who was appointed Lieutenant of Dungiven Castle in 1604. The portion of Derry containing Dungiven fell at the Plantation to the Skinner's Company, whose grant from the Irish Society is dated March the 22nd, 1617. In an account of Skinner's Hall, *alias* Dungiven, in 1618 it is described as including a strong castle, two and a half stories high, with a large bawn of stone well fortified. As the enclosure now stands it has three sides, the present castle forming the fourth and south side, with entrance gateways on the north, east, and west sides. The east and west sides of the bawn are about 150 ft. from the castle to the rear, the north side of the bawn is about 200 ft. long.

There is another bawn at Brackfield, about 8 miles from Derry, in this case the enclosure is some 70 ft.

square ; the southern side was closed by a house, about
17 ft. wide and extending the whole length of the side.
The western side was probably occupied by offices, so
that there would have been an open court about 42 ft.
square on the north-eastern quarter of the bawn. The
wall was defended on the outside by two circular flanking
towers, one at the north-west, and the other at the
south-east, corner. The gate was on the northern side
of the enclosure.

It has been calculated that there are 122 crannogs
known in Ulster,[1] but in addition to these there are
probably many more which have not yet been recorded.
Fermanagh heads the list with some 39, while there
are 20 in Antrim and 19 in Monaghan. Lisnacroghera
Crannog, Co. Antrim, the most interesting of these, is
the most important crannog hitherto found in Ireland.
It lies at a little distance from Broughshane, parish of
Skerry, Barony of Antrim. It was discovered in 1882
by workmen when cutting turf, who found the oaken
timbers of the structure laid in regular order ; unfortun-
ately most of these were removed before any expert
had seen them, though a few of the piles remained in
position. The antiquities found in the crannog were
remarkable, they belonged to the La Tène or Late
Celtic period, and included some beautifully decorated
bronze sword-sheaths, an iron sword, some bronze
spear ferules, one of which was discovered attached to
the shaft of a spear ; and other objects.

Other interesting crannogs in this province are those
of Ballydoolough, Co. Fermanagh, Lough Eyes in the
same county, and Cloneygonnell in Co. Cavan. Bally-

[1] Wood-Martin, *Lake Dwellings of Ireland*, 1886.

Sword-sheaths from
Lisnacroghera
Crannog

doolough Crannog is 5 miles from Enniskillen. It is situated in a lake, the waters of which cover about 24 acres. In 1870, a small island was discovered, upon which were found fragments of pottery. This led to an examination of the site, and an oaken beam was found near the centre of the island, nearly 16 ft. long, which had been the lower part of one side of a dwelling ; when clearing the site, the framework of the house was discovered, it consisted of beams of oak, grooved and mortised, with the corners dovetailed and secured with wooden pins. The kitchen midden of the inhabitants was found to contain numerous fragments of pottery, and bones of pig, cow, deer, and horse. The antiquities found included some iron knife-blades, a crucible, a brooch, portion of a quern, etc.

Lough Eyes Crannog is situated about 2 miles north-east of the village of Lisbellaw, and measures about two-thirds by a quarter of a mile. In 1870 the summer was exceptionally dry, and six small islands were exposed. The most important crannog of the group measures some 208 ft. in circumference. It is built up of a layer of branches of oak, alder, pine, hazel, etc. mixed with brambles resting on about 6 ft. of peat overlying a deposit of sand and marl. The floor was composed of earth and stones resting on the branches. The stockading which originally surrounded the island was also found. At a later period the remains of a piled causeway, which had connected together the islands in the Lough, was discovered. The remains on the principal and other crannogs consisted of a large number of fragments of pottery vessels, whetstones, querns, etc., with a large quantity of bones of domestic animals.

Cloneygonnell, in the parish of Kilmore, contained three crannogs which were discovered when Toneymore Lough had been drained, but it was only when the largest

Arboe High Cross, Co. Tyrone

of the crannogs had been cut through for the railway that the site was examined. It was found that the largest crannog was surrounded with piles arranged in two circles, it was composed of a floor of ashes, stones, bones, and clay, resting on horizontal planks of oak and branches of hazel, etc., overlying peat. The planks were surrounded outside by a circle of trunks of oak, these being held in place by the stockades. Among the antiquities discovered were querns, a mortar, whetstones, combs, bronze-pins, pottery-fragments, and several iron implements.

HIGH CROSSES

There are some 30 decorated High Crosses in Ulster. Of these the fine monument at Arboe, Cookstown, Co. Tyrone (p. 121), which is 18½ ft. in height and elaborately carved with panels depicting Biblical scenes, is remarkable. The Inishowen peninsular, Co. Donegal, contains a series of early crosses and slabs; those at Carndonagh and Fahan are also worthy of study.

ARCHITECTURE

Monastic Foundations

Ware (1654) gives a list of nearly fifty religious establishments of various kinds that formerly flourished in the province of Ulster. Some of these were small and unimportant, and all traces of them have disappeared. Taken as a whole, the remains of ecclesiastical buildings in Ulster are not of so interesting a description as those of the other provinces. But in the county of Down there are some well-preserved remains such as those of Grey Abbey; the Abbey of Inch; the Abbey Church (now portion of the Cathedral) of Downpatrick; and Newtownards Priory.

Grey Abbey, situated in the village of Grey Abbey, on Strangford Lough, Co. Down, the most picturesque of the ecclesiastical buildings remaining in the province, was founded in A.D. 1193 by Affreca, the wife of John de Courcy, and colonised by Cistercian monks from the Abbey of Holm Cultram in Cumberland. It was dedicated to the Virgin Mary. Its Irish name was *Mainistir Liath*, the Grey Monastery; in early records it is referred to as *De Jugo Dei in Ultonia*. The ruins consist of the church and conventual buildings. The church is cruciform in plan, and most of its walls are standing; it consists of an aisleless nave, chancel, and transepts, with a square tower at the junction of the nave and chancel. The transepts have eastern chapels. The conventual buildings are on the south of the church: they are in a ruinous condition, but their foundations can easily be traced: they comprise the sacristy, chapter house, calefactory, with the monk's dorter above it, kitchen, refectory, and buttery. The cloister garth is much damaged, but appears to have been oblong in plan. A number of mediæval masons' marks can be seen incised upon fragments of building stones and the walls of the building. The architecture of the abbey appears to belong as a whole to the thirteenth century, but there are some traces of Romanesque work. The convent was dissolved in A.D. 1541 when some of its possessions were granted to Gerald earl of Kildare. A curious leaden matrix of a seal of Ralph Irton bishop of Carlisle A.D. 1280–1291 was discovered in 1842 when clearing out the foundations of the ruins of Grey Abbey. The matrix is probably a contemporary forgery, as lead is

an unusual material for the seal of a bishop. As an
explanation of the presence of the matrix at Grey Abbey
it may be stated that Grey Abbey was an affiliated cell
of the Abbey of Holm Cultram in Cumberland in the
diocese of Carlisle. A certain Ralph, who was first,
Abbot of Grey Abbey, and afterwards, of Holm Cultram, subsequently became Bishop of Carlisle. An entry
of A.D. 1222 refers to the promotion of Ralph to the
Abbotship of Holm Cultram from Grey Abbey. If, therefore, it be assumed that Ralph entered the monastery
at a very early age and lived to be over ninety, it would
account for the presence of his seal-matrix at Grey
Abbey.

Newtownards priory was founded by Walter de
Burgo earl of Ulster, in A.D. 1244, being dedicated to
St Columba, and occupied by Friars Preachers (Domini-
cans). It was a foundation of some importance, and
provincial chapters of the Order were held in it in 1298
and 1312. At the dissolution of the monasteries it was
surrendered to Henry VIII.'s commissioners by the last
prior, Patrick O'Doran. The priory and its lands were
granted by King James I. to James, Viscount Clandeboy,
and were afterwards assigned to Hugh, Viscount Mont-
gomery of the Ards. Nothing now remains of the conventual buildings but the church. This consists of a nave
and north aisle with a tower, which projects from the
centre of its external wall. There are some traces of a
chancel. The nave is the only remaining portion of the
church which dates from the foundation. The west and
south walls are fairly preserved, and there is some interesting fifteenth-century work in the nave arcade.
The tower, which is later than either the nave or aisles,
belongs to the Jacobean period.

The only remaining portions of the Abbey church at Down, are now embodied in the cathedral of Downpatrick. The Abbey was founded in 1186 by John de Courcy for Benedictine monks, and the modern cathedral, commenced in 1790, was grafted on to the remains of the eastern arm of the Abbey church. The remains of the Abbey to be noticed are some capitals in the nave arcades, and some mouldings in other portions of the building, which belong to the Gothic period ; some fragments of Irish Romanesque work are also to be seen. The nave and transepts of the church, and the conventual buildings have disappeared, but their foundations are probably buried under the ground of the neighbouring fields and gardens.

Inch Abbey was founded by John de Courcy in 1180 for Cistercian monks. The ruins are attractive, but not extensive; there is little left of the church except the chancel, the windows of which are in the style of the thirteenth century.

The remains of the monastery of Saul, Co. Down, are scanty ; the site is, however, interesting as it commemorates by its position and name (*Sabhall*=a barn), the place where Christianity was first preached in Ireland. When St Patrick landed near Downpatrick in A.D. 432 he preached to the lord of the soil, Dichu, and his people, in a barn. A church was later erected on the same site, and a monastery for Regular Canons was founded, which was restored in the twelfth century by Malachias Ó Morghair bishop of Down. The greater portion of the church has now disappeared, but there is a small cell in the churchyard said to be the tomb of Bishop Ó Morghair.

About half-a-mile beyond the eastern end of the

town of Newtownards are the ruins of the once famous monastery of Movilla. The extant remains consist merely of the gables, and portions of the side walls of the ancient church, into which are built an interesting series of Anglo-Norman slabs. They are of the usual type with a floriated cross; some bear a sword showing them to be monuments of knights, others bear shears for a lady. There is one slab with an Irish inscription to Dertriu, who is supposed to have been Abbot of Movilla in the tenth century. The ruins of the church at present to be seen probably belong to the fifteenth century. The original foundation is reputed to date from about A.D. 550, the monastery having been founded by St Finnian for Augustinian Canons.

The monastery at Donegal is of peculiar interest from its connection with the celebrated *Annals of Donegal*, better known as the *Annals of the Four Masters*, which were compiled in the monastery between A.D. 1632 and 1636. The names of the four scribes of these *Annals* were Michael, Conary, and Cucogry, O'Clery and Ferfeasa O'Mulconry. The *Annals* cover a period of 4500 years ending in A.D. 1616. The ruins of the monastery include the remains of a cruciform church, and seven arches of the cloister on the north side. The convent was founded for Franciscans in 1473 by Aodh Ruadh Ó Domhnaill (Hugh Roe O'Donel), and his wife, a daughter of Conchobhair Ó Briain of Thomond.

The celebrated inscribed silver shrine of the *Cathach* belonged to the O'Donels. One of the six early Irish Book-Shrines that have been preserved, it was made between A.D. 1062 and 1098, by order of Cathbarr Ó Domhnaill (head of the clan of which St Columba of Iona was a member) and Domhnall Mac Robartaigh, coarb of Kells, by Sitric, one of a family of artificers who had some connection with the monastery of Kells, to enshrine a Psalter, which there seems good reason to believe was written by St Columba.[1]

This Psalter was formerly carried into battle before the hosts of the O'Donels for whom it was supposed to

The " Cathach " Shrine (front)

secure victory. On this account it was called the *Cathach* or battler. The shrine was repaired on several occasions, and the present lid is of fourteenth-century date. It was taken to France by Brigadier Daniel O'Donel in the early part of the eighteenth century, whence it was obtained after his death by Sir Neal

[1] See Lawlor, *Proc. Royal Irish Academy*, xxxiii., sec. C, pp. 241-443.

O'Donel, Bart. At present it is deposited, together with the MS., in the Library of the Royal Irish Academy.

Some ecclesiastical remains are to be seen on the Island of Tory, Co. Donegal, where a monastery is reputed to have been founded by St Columba before he went to Scotland. The principal object of antiquity now remaining is the round tower, which measures about 51 ft. in height. There is also upon the island a monolithic Tau cross, 6 ft. in height, made of a thick slab of mica slate.

Devenish Island, in Lough Erne, Co. Fermanagh, contains some interesting ecclesiastical remains, associated chiefly with St Molaise, whose silver shrine is now preserved in the Royal Irish Academy's collection in the National Museum. The Saint was educated under St Finnian at the great school of Clonard. The monastery of Devenish was founded about 541 A.D. : the present remains consist of a small rectangular oratory known as St Molaise's house ; a round tower, 84 ft. in height, with a remarkable cornice having four human heads sculptured on it ; the so-called " Great Church," which appears to have formed the southern wing of a monastery ; and the tower and ruins of the side walls of St Mary's Abbey. This group of antiquities also includes a High Cross, having a shaft elaborately carved with ornament of the Tudor period ; the present head of the cross does not appear to be the original one.

The shrine of St Molaise, in the National Museum collection referred to above, was made to contain a copy of the gospels belonging to the Saint, but the MS. is no longer extant. The shrine is in the form of a small box measuring 5¼ in. by 3½ in. by 4½ in. It is made up of five bronze plates covered with ornamental plates of silver. The design on the front of the shrine is in the form

The Shrine of St Molaise (front)

of an Irish cross, the outer quarters of which contain the symbols of the four Evangelists. On the bottom of the case is an inscription in Irish which translated reads : " A prayer for Cennfaelad, the successor of

u I

Molaise, by whom this case was made, for . . . and
for Gilla Báithín, the artisan who did the work."

A remarkable antiquity to be mentioned in connection
with Lough Erne is the so-called Lough Erne Shrine. One
of the earliest reliquaries that up to the present has been
discovered in Ireland, it is probably of eighth century
date.   It was fished out of Lough Erne about half way
between Belleek and Enniskillen in 1891.   The shrine,
which contained a smaller box, is in the form of a small
house with a gabled roof; it consists of a box of yew
wood covered with bronze plates which seem to have
been tinned: the sides are decorated with circular
medallions having amber centres surrounded by inter-
laced work.   It is preserved in the Royal Irish Academy's
collection in the National Museum, Dublin.

A curious ecclesiastical antiquity in this province is
a narrow, deep cave situated on a rocky island in Lough
Derg ; this cave is the famous " Purgatory of St Patrick."
Local tradition relates that the island in which the cave
is situated was regarded with terror by the inhabitants
as an abode of evil spirits, and that St Patrick passing
through the district determined to free the people from
their fears.   He therefore landed on the island, entered
the cave, and continued there in prayer for about forty
days.   At length he emerged, having succeeded not
only in driving away the devil from his last stronghold
in Ireland, but also in having been permitted to see
the pains by which sin is expiated in Purgatory.   St
Patrick's Purgatory enjoyed much repute in the Middle
Ages.   Giraldus Cambrensis alludes to it in his Topography of Ireland, placing the island of Lough Derg
among the marvels of Ireland.   Froissart described it
from an account given to him by Sir William Lisle who

had visited it.   Henry of Saltrey a Benedictine monk of
Saltrey in Huntingdonshire in the reign of Henry II.
wrote an account of the visit of a knight named Owen
to the cave.   The Purgatory is mentioned by Matthew
of Paris in his history, and early found its way into
Italian literature.   It became a well-known subject
for popular books in Spain and France.   Numerous
pilgrims from various parts of Europe, many of high
rank, visited the Purgatory.   In 1497 the cave was
closed by the order of the Pope, who had received a
hostile account of it from a Dutch monk.   But pilgrims
continued to flock to the cave from all parts of Europe ;
and in 1503 the Archbishop of Armagh appealed to
Pope Pius III. to withdraw the prohibition of Alex-
ander VI. ; a Papal Bull was accordingly issued granting
liberal indulgences to pilgrims visiting the sacred spot.
A monastery had been founded in very early times in
Lough Derg, on an island close to that in which the cave
was situated, and had shared in the celebrity of the spot.
In 1632 the Government having decided to stop the
pilgrimages, destroyed the monastic buildings.   This
attempt was unsuccessful.   In Queen Anne's reign an Act
of Parliament constituted all pilgrimages to St Patrick's
Purgatory unlawful assemblies punishable with a fine,
but the pilgrimages still continued.   During the last fifty
years a modern monastery has been built with a Hospice
for the accommodation of pilgrims, which many persons
visit each year.   The pilgrimage opens yearly on
the 1st of June and closes on August the 15th.   Mr
Baring-Gould devotes an article in *Curious Myths of
the Middle Ages* to St Patrick's Purgatory ; he concludes
that the story is founded on the ancient myths of
descents into Hell prevalent among many peoples.   The

descents of Herakles, Orpheus, Odysseus, and Aeneas, are classical instances, while many others occur in the mythologies of different races.

Cathedrals

There are nine cathedral churches [1] in the province of Ulster, *i.e.* Armagh, Clogher, Conor, Derry, Down, Dromore, Kilmore, Lisburn, and Raphoe. None of these buildings are of much architectural interest, nearly all being comparatively modern.

The Cathedral of Armagh (*Ard-Macha*, Macha's height), about which, as the first church here erected, romance must always linger, was founded and given its pre-eminent position by St Patrick, is a small and almost entirely modern building. It was restored about 1840 by Archbishop Beresford, when the few remains of ancient building, which had till then escaped, were obliterated ; it occupies a delightful site on the summit of a hill overlooking the town. The body of King Brian Boraimhe, the victor of Clontarf, was brought to Armagh after the battle and buried within the cathedral.

Clogher (a place abounding in stones), in Co. Tyrone, is a small village, on the line of railway between Omagh and Enniskillen. The bishopric is said to have been founded by St Patrick. The present cathedral was erected about 1740 in the mediæval style, but was remodelled as a classical building in 1818.

Connor (originally *Doire nagcon*, the oakwood of the wild dogs), a village near Ballymena, Co. Antrim, is an old ecclesiastical foundation dating from the latter

---

[1] The writer has received assistance in writing these short notes on the Cathedrals from *The Cathedral Churches of Ireland*, 1894, by the late T. M. Fallow., F.S.A.

end of the fifth century ; the existing cathedral is an ordinary modern country church with no features of interest.

The present cathedral of Derry (*Doire*=an oak-wood), was commenced in 1628 and finished in 1633. The cost of the building was defrayed by the Corporation of the city of London, it amounted to some £4000. Built in the perpendicular style, it is interesting as a specimen of the Gothic of that period. In the early portion of last century a new tower and spire were built ; a chancel has recently been erected.

Down (a fort), this See was founded about the close of the fifth century. St Patrick is stated to have been buried here. In A.D. 1186 John de Courcy restored the church, changing its name from Holy Trinity, and rededicating it to St Patrick. Benedictine monks were introduced there from St Werburg's monastery in Chester ; until 1541 the prior and convent formed the bishop's chapter. In 1538 Lord Grey, the Lord Deputy, burned the cathedral, for which and other crimes he was.executed in 1541. The present cathedral incorporates a few remains of the ancient building, but it is for the most part modern, having been rebuilt at the end of the eighteenth and commencement of the nineteenth centuries.

Dromore (the great ridge) is a bishopric of considerable antiquity, having been founded early in the sixth century. The ancient cathedral was destroyed in the rebellion of the seventeenth century : the present edifice was built by Jeremy Taylor, bishop of Down and Connor, who held this See *in commendam*. Jeremy Taylor's building appears to have been a plain oblong church with a square, plain tower at the west end. It has been restored within recent years ; an apse has been added to the east end, and on the north side an aisle.

The Cathedral of Kilmore (the great church) is quite modern, having been built about 1860. It is a small church of cruciform shape with a central tower surmounted by a small spire.

Lisburn Cathedral owes its origin to Charles II., who in 1662 constituted the parish church of Lisburn the cathedral church of Down and Conner ; the cathedral churches of both these places being at that time in ruins. It is an uninteresting church planned as a parallelogram.

Raphoe Cathedral is a cruciform church with a tall square western tower. It does not show any signs of age, but possibly contains some ancient portions built into the walls. Raphoe is a corruption of *Raith-both,* the fort of the huts.

Castles

There is hardly any portion of Ireland containing so many castles as the shores of Lecale and Strangford Lough. In Co. Antrim the castles were perched on the basalt crags which fringed the coast from Carrickfergus to Dunluce and Dunseverick.

The most interesting of these Anglo-Norman castles is that of Dundrum, Co. Down, which has recently been identified with the *Castrum de Rath* mentioned in records of the thirteenth century. It was erected by John de Courcy on a rocky elevation on the site of *Dun Rudhraighe*, an ancient Celtic fort, in which was held, according to tradition, the *Fled Bricrend*, the feast of Bricriu, which forms the subject of a well-known Middle-Irish tale. The tower of Dundrum is probably the most perfect example of a donjon in Ireland. It

is a cylindrical shell of masonry, with an external
diameter of 45 ft., the walls are 8 ft. thick, and the tower
measures 43 ft. in height. The basement chamber of
the donjon is cut out of the rock. A moat quarried
out of the solid rock partially surrounds the donjon.
A portion of the original wall round the courtyard is
still standing : on the southern slope of the hill are the
ruins of an Elizabethan house.

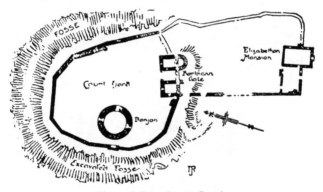

Plan of Dundrum Castle

Carrickfergus Castle occupies a commanding position
on a rock 30 ft. high, and overlooks the lough. The
date of its erection is uncertain, though the thirteenth
century may be suggested as a likely time for this to
have taken place. Edward Bruce made it his chief
residence during his expedition in Ireland : at a later
period it was occupied by General Schomberg. The
stone on which, according to tradition, William III.
first set foot in Ireland is quite close to the castle. The
great keep of the castle is a square tower 90 ft. high

with walls 9 ft. thick.   The building is now used as an
armoury and military store.

Dunluce Castle is a romantic ruin occupying the whole
of a detached basaltic rock.   There are the remains of

Chimney-piece in Donegal Castle

the entrance barbican and two towers : the residential
buildings include the Great Hall, 70 ft. by 23 ft., and
another large apartment with bedrooms over these.
The castle was probably erected by the MacQuillans,
who were in occupation when the MacDonnels came

over from Scotland after their surrender of the lordship
of the Isles to James IV. in 1476.

The Castle of the O'Donels at Donegal is, as it at present
stands, a Jacobean building, erected by Sir Basil Brooke
in 1610 ; but it contains the remains of the older castle,
which consist of a tall tower with two turrets.   In the
principal apartment is a fine chimney-piece carved
with the arms of Brooke, and of Brooke impaling
Leicester of Toft.

Kilbarron Castle near Ballyshannon, Co. Donegal,
is now in ruins : formerly a fortress of the O'Clerys,
it stands on a cliff overhanging the sea.

The port of Ardglass, Co. Down, was of much importance at the time of the Anglo-Norman invasion of Ireland,
and no less than seven castles were built there by de
Courcy.   But the remains of castles now to be seen in
this locality are of considerably later date ; the best
preserved of these, formerly known as Jordan's Castle, is
situated near the Quay.   It is supposed to be named
after Jordan de Saukvill.   The castle was besieged for
a long period during the Earl of Tyrone's rebellion.
The present remains consist of a lofty tower, 70 ft. in
height, which is maintained in excellent order by its
present owner, Mr F. J. Bigger.

The Savages of the Ards peninsula, Co. Down, were
the great castle builders of this region, and ruins of
some of their numerous strongholds still exist.   At
Portaferry there are the remains of what must have
been a strong fortress.   It consists at present of a
rectangular keep, and belongs to the present representative of the Savage family, Major-General Nugent.

Another ruin of interest is Kirkistone Castle, Bally-
halbert, which was built by Roland Savage early in the

seventeenth century.   The keep, which is still perfect, is
in the centre of a square enclosure, the southern wall of
which is flanked by a circular tower at each corner.   This

Jordan's Castle, now called Castle Shane,
Ardglass, Co. Down

building is remarkable as being one of the few castles in the
Ards district in which the courtyard has been preserved.
The remains of several castles may be seen in the
neighbourhood of Strangford Lough, practically all are

of Anglo-Norman origin; now they are mostly in a ruinous condition.

Doe Castle, Fanad, Co. Donegal, was formerly the chief seat of MacSuibhne na dTuath (MacSwiney of the Tuatha). It is situated on a low rocky point defended on three sides by the sea, and on the fourth by a ditch; it consists of a strong central tower some 55 ft. in height, surrounded by a battlemented enclosure. The castle was converted into a modern residence and occupied until recent times, but it has maintained the features of a sixteenth-century fortress. The MacSwineys who built this castle were brought into Tirconnell from Scotland by the O'Donels. The celebrated Hugh Roe O'Donel (Aodh Ruadh Ó Domhnaill) was a foster son of Eoghan óg MacSuibhne, and probably much of his youth was spent at Doe Castle.

ADMINISTRATION

THE province of Ulster is the most populous of the four. According to the census of 1911 its total population was 1,581,696. It includes the two large County Boroughs of Belfast and Londonderry, and may be said to be the industrial province, although it is by no means unimportant from the point of view of agriculture. Under the Government of Ireland Act, 1920, the counties of Antrim, Armagh, Down, Fermanagh, Londonderry, and Tyrone come under the Government of Northern Ireland, the remaining three counties of Donegal, Monaghan and Cavan, coming under the Government of Southern Ireland. The population, area, etc., of the larger administrative areas are set out in the following table:

(1)	Popu-lation (Census of 1911). (2)	Area on which the Valuations have been deter-mined. (3)	Valua-tion on 1st March 1914. (4)	Number of Mem-bers of Parlia-ment. (See Note.) (5)
		Acres.	£	
County Boroughs				
Belfast . .	386,947	16,476	1,576,116	4
Londonderry .	40,780	2,311	114,565	1
MARITIME COUNTIES				
Down				
Rural Districts	157,561	602,713	696,332	} 5
Urban Districts	46,742	5,962	153,505	
Antrim (A)				
Rural Districts .	148,817	696,014	610,403	} 4
Urban Districts	45,316	5,528	136,142	
Londonderry (B)				
Rural Districts	87,665	517,884	296,488	} 2
Urban Districts	11,911	1,586	29,687	
Donegal				
Rural Districts	162,379	1,195,186	302,824	} 4
Urban Districts	6,158	2,256	9,724	
INLAND COUNTIES				
Armagh				
Rural Districts	85,812	309,786	356,890	} 3
Urban Districts	34,479	2,867	89,023	
Monaghan				
Rural Districts	61,026	317,606	255,352	} 2
Urban Districts	10,429	1,208	22,593	
Cavan				
Rural Districts	85,291	464,937	265,416	} 2
Urban Districts	5,882	2,085	14,747	
Fermanagh				
Rural Districts	56,989	417,391	228,801	} 2
Urban Districts	4,847	317	14,343	
Tyrone				
Rural Districts	125,207	776,299	419,383	} 4
Urban Districts	17,458	3,387	48,481	

NOTE. The boundaries of Parliamentary Divisions are not coterminous with local administrative areas.

(A). The boundaries of the Urban District of Portrush were extended in 1915 at the expense of the Rural Districts of Ballymoney (County Antrim) and Coleraine (County Londonderry). The figures given include the increased population of the town, in Column 2, but the old Area and Valuation in Columns 3 and 4.

(B). Portstewart was constituted an Urban District on April 1st, 1916. It is included with the Urban Districts in Column 2, as regards Population, but with the Rural Districts in Columns 3 and 4, as regards Area and Valuation.

Of the county areas all that it is necessary to say as to their general administration is that they form part of the system of Local Government administered through County and Urban District Councils, Rural Councils and Boards of Guardians as explained in the volume for Ireland (General). It is, however, necessary to say something of the administration of the great and flourishing industrial capital of Ireland, and the highly organised administrative system which finds its centre in the magnificent City Hall which, begun in 1898, was opened in 1906. The first Corporation for Belfast was elected in 1833, the population at that time being slightly over 74,000. Its home was a small and inconvenient building, which was rented, in Victoria Square. In 1871 the population had increased to 170,000 and new buildings were provided in Victoria Street. Only £16,000 was available for the purpose and as it was necessary to provide a Town Hall, Municipal Offices, Recorders' and Justices' Courts it soon became necessary to open negotiations in regard to the present building, which is adequate to the needs of this great industrial and commercial centre. The site of the present building was occupied by the old White Linen Hall, and in this was housed the Linen

Hall Library, which was conducted by the Belfast Library and Society for Promoting Knowledge. The present building was designed by Mr (now Sir) A. Brumwell Thomas, of Westminster, and built by Messrs H. and J. Martin, Ltd., of Belfast.

Belfast became a County Borough in 1899 under the Local Government (Ireland) Act of 1898. Its Lord Mayor, Aldermen, and Councillors have wide powers and responsibilities which they discharge through numerous committees and Corporation officials whose offices are for the most part in the City Hall.

The Public Library (controlled by the Technical Instruction and Library Committee) is a fine building in Royal Avenue. The lending library contains over 32,000 volumes, while an interesting Museum and Art Gallery is situated on the third floor. The extensive business connected with the port of Belfast is entrusted to the Harbour Board which is elected by the ratepayers, and is representative of the merchants, shippers and shipowners of the city. Its offices in Corporation Square adjoin the docks.

Customs, Inland Revenue, and other Government business is carried on in a large Government building at the foot of High Street adjacent to Donegal Quay, in which is also located the Local Marine Board.

Londonderry is the only other County Borough in the province. Its original name as anglicised was *Derry* the prefix *London* being added by charter of James I. in 1613 on the incorporation of the Irish Society, who colonised the district. It received other charters from Oliver Cromwell, Charles II. and James II. It stood under the Local Government Act of 1898 in the same position as Belfast, and was given a separate

lieutenancy, shrievalty, and other corresponding privi-
leges. The city is divided into ten wards, each returning
one Alderman and three Councillors to the County
Borough Council. Here, in common with the rest of
Ireland, the principle of Proportional Representation was
in the elections for 1920 applied to Municipal Elections.

EDUCATION

Belfast has now its own university, which may be
regarded as a university for Ulster. Under the administration of Sir Robert Peel, the Government in the year
1845 placed an Act on the Statute Book providing for
the establishment of three Queen's Colleges in Belfast,
Cork, and Galway. These colleges (opened in 1849)
established to meet an urgent need, were yet received
with deep mistrust. Five years later the " Queen's
University of Ireland " was founded, and its charter
gave powers for the conferring of degrees on the students
of the three Queen's Colleges, but in the following year
a plenary Synod of the Catholic Hierarchy held at
Thurles condemned the new Queen's Colleges as " dangerous to faith and morals," and in 1854 a Catholic University of Ireland was founded. In 1879 the Queen's
University was replaced by the Royal University of
Ireland which was an examining institution with which
the University College of Dublin (which absorbed the
Catholic University) was affiliated. This University
College and the three Queen's Colleges of Belfast, Cork,
and Galway presented students for the degrees of the
Royal University of Ireland, to the examinations for
which external candidates were also admitted. This
arrangement, wholly inadequate and unsatisfactory
as it was, persisted until the Irish Universities' Act of

1908 provided for the establishment of two universities —the National University of Ireland and the Queen's University of Belfast. This latter naturally occupies the picturesque buildings which had been provided for Queen's College. But up to 1905 the equipment of the institution was grievously inadequate. To provide

Queen's University, Belfast

the much-needed extensions, however, the citizens raised £100,000 for the erection of laboratories and the endowment of new Chairs. In addition, a splendid hostel for lady students has been built and endowed at a cost of about £70,000.

The university possesses a fine library and museums. It has faculties of Arts, Science, Law, Commerce, and Medicine, and has schemes of co-ordination with the Royal College of Science for Ireland and the Municipal

St Louis' Convent, Monaghan, an important Girls' Secondary School

College of Technology. Many private benefactors have endowed scholarships and prizes.

The medical school is one of the largest in the United Kingdom, and in the year 1919 it had no fewer than 543 students on its roll. It works in connection with the Royal Victoria Hospital, the Mater Hospital and other hospitals in the city.

The university has on its staff 25 professors, 24 lecturers, and a large staff of assistants and demonstrators. The Parliamentary Register contains about 3000 names.

The Methodist College, a theological college for the training of candidates for the Wesleyan ministry, is also a secondary school with splendid equipment, providing education both for boys and girls. The Victoria College, with which the name of Mrs Byers will always be associated, provides higher education for girls. Campbell College, situated some three miles from the city, was completed in 1894 ; it is a residential school for boys, and has splendid buildings and equipment. Among the principal schools of secondary character for Catholic boys is St Malachy's College, situated in the Antrim Road.

In the field of technical education very remarkable progress has been made in recent years. Prior to 1900, while much excellent work was done in scattered and inadequate buildings, there was a serious lack of funds. Governmental assistance was limited to the grants made by the English Board of Education (the Science and Art Department of South Kensington), who had one science inspector—the late Professor Preston, F.R.S. —resident in Dublin. The provision was totally inadequate, but on the establishment in Ireland of the Department of Agriculture and Technical Instruction, a sum of nearly £11,000 per annum was made available, besides Treasury grants made on a capitation basis and the product of the rate. The Act establishing the Department conferred the power to raise a rate for technical education of a penny in the pound, and power was conferred by the earlier Technical Instruction Act (1889) to raise another penny. The Corporation did not delay to make the necessary provision. Representatives of the shipbuilding, textile, and other trades were invited to co-operate, and great enthusiasm and interest was manifested. A Principal was appointed, and a most suitable site found in front of the Academical Institution in College Square East. The committee estimated for a building to cost £57,000, and Mr Sam Stevenson, C.E., a local architect, proceeded to prepare plans. But before the building was commenced the great growth in the number of students indicated that the scheme was not sufficiently comprehensive, and the plans were revised for a building to cost £81,000. During the erection of this it became evident that it would be still inadequate to the needs, and now a fifth storey was added, bringing up the cost to about £100,000. The beautiful building was opened by His Excellency the Earl of Aberdeen in October 1907. The number of students grew rapidly and the enrolment is now over 7000.

The College provides day and evening courses of instruction, the latter including science, engineering, textiles, various trade subjects, notably in the group of subjects concerned with architecture and building, women's work (domestic economy, dressmaking, hygiene, sick-nursing, etc.), horticulture and allotment gardening. The Art Department specialises in design as applied to industries, at the same time providing a general art education of a high character.

A notable feature of the College is the Day Trades' Preparatory School which provides a general and scientific training for boys who propose to enter a trade.

Municipal College of Technology, Belfast

It may be added that this school, though undenominational, is attended largely by Protestants, while a school of similar type, attended mainly by Catholics, has been organised by the Christian Brothers in Hardinge Street. Both of these schools are very successful and are supported very largely by special grants from the Department of Agriculture and Technical Instruction.

An interesting development, full of great promise, was initiated a few years ago by the National Teachers of Belfast who, acting in co-operation with the College, have established a leaving examination, the certificate for which is recognised for entrance to the College.

On the equipment of the science, engineering, and other laboratories the committee expended over £40,000, and there is a large staff of professors and other teachers. Here, as elsewhere, efforts are made, with gratifying success, to co-operate with local trades and industries, and accommodation has been provided for a Textile Testing House which performs important services to the textile industry. There is, moreover, an admirable scheme of co-ordination with Queen's University.

There is no lack in Belfast of secondary schools both for boys and girls, some of which have been mentioned already. It is interesting to recall the fact that what is known as the Belfast Academical Institution, now a well-known secondary school of the first rank, was opened by the Presbyterians in 1814, and became the General Assembly's Theological College.

Londonderry, though much smaller, has displayed great enthusiasm for education. Up to 1908 a School of Art and some classes in science and technology were conducted in the old Town Hall at the head of Shipquay Street, but in that year an excellent new building was provided and, to the evening classes in science, art, and numerous technological subjects was added a Day Trades' Preparatory School. The progress of this school has been very marked. Not far away is the premier Protestant boys' secondary school of the city— Foyle College—and in the same neighbourhood is the Victoria High School, close to which is " Northlands "—

a school built by the Department and conducted by the Victoria High School under their direction. The object of Northlands is to confer a training in household management for girls who have already received a good

Municipal Technical School, Londonderry

secondary education. The conditions approximate as far as may be to those of home life.

The M'Crea Magee College, affiliated with Trinity College, Dublin, is for the purpose of training Presbyterian ministers.

INDUSTRIES & MANUFACTURES

THE north-eastern province is the most populous and the most industrialised, but manufactures are chiefly carried on in that portion of the area which lies to the east of the Bann and Lough Neagh, that is to say in Antrim and Down. Nevertheless there are important linen industries in the counties of Londonderry, Tyrone, and Armagh.

One cannot think of Ulster without recalling the vast significance of her two principal industries—shipbuilding and linen manufacture. Their progress and present status are so interwoven with the greatness of Belfast and its surrounding districts that some account of their history and present position is called for.

Although small shipbuilding industries have been started in Londonderry and Larne, the fame of the industry centres round the great firms of Messrs Harland & Wolff, and Messrs Workman, Clark & Co., of Belfast.

Shipbuilding as an industry began in Belfast in the latter part of the eighteenth century.[1] The earliest record of shipbuilding, however, dates from 1636, when a number of Presbyterians of Belfast built the *Eagle Wing*, a vessel of 150 tons register, on the shore of Belfast Lough in order to seek refuge in the New World. It was driven back by heavy weather. In 1682 the

[1] For many of the facts in this account the writer is indebted to Professor C. H. Oldham's paper on " The History of Belfast Shipbuilding," read before the Statistical and Social Inquiry Society of Ireland in December 1910.

largest vessel owned in Belfast was the *Antelope* a Virginian trader of 200 tons. In 1699 the *Loyal Charles*, of 250 tons, was launched, but there was no regular place for building ships in Belfast until ninety years later. The brothers William and Hugh Ritchie from Ayrshire began to build ships on the Lagan in 1791. The former, the real pioneer, is known as " the father of Belfast shipbuilding." Few ships, however, were built in Belfast until after 1824, when the intro- duction of steam-power as a means of propulsion and Free Trade between Ireland and Great Britain provided a stimulus under which a shipyard was established at " Ritchie's Dock," filled up in 1849 and now forming Corporation Square. Progress was impeded by the state of the Lagan, and vessels larger than about 300 tons burden were unable to get through the channel. Harbour Commissioners were, however, appointed in 1847 with full powers and control of the port, and improved conditions were secured. The first steamship built in Ireland was the *Chieftain*, which was constructed by Messrs Ritchie & MacLaine in 1826, the engines (of 70 horse-power) being supplied by Messrs Coates & Young. She was of 200 tons burden. Though the *Seagull*, the first iron ship built in Belfast, was launched in 1844, the business of iron shipbuilding dates from 1853, when Messrs Robert Hickson & Co. took ground on the artificial piece of land known as Queen's Island, and opened a new shipbuilding yard. The *Mary Stenhouse*, a sailing vessel of 1289 tons register, was launched in 1854. This year marks the coming to Belfast of a man who was destined to found the great firm of Harland & Wolff. Messrs Hickson had found it necessary to dismiss their manager and advertise

Shipyards, Belfast

for another. The successful applicant for the post was Edward James Harland, of Scarborough. Harland had served an apprenticeship with Robert Stephenson & Co., of Newcastle-on-Tyne. He became a journeyman at 20s. per week, and afterwards a manager, and was but twenty-three years of age when he became manager at Queen's Island. He appreciated the scope of his opportunities, and in the face of very great difficulties " won through." He later, with the assistance of a friend, purchased Mr Hickson's interest in the works, and acquired orders for three steamers from Messrs John Bibby, Sons & Co., of Liverpool. At this time Mr Harland had in his drawing office a young draughtsman named Wolff who had served his apprenticeship with Messrs Whitworth, of Manchester. The steamers were completed, the works prospered, Mr Wolff was taken into partnership, and so started in 1862 the world-famed firm of Harland & Wolff.

It was the excellence and efficiency of the vessels of this firm that led to the promotion of the Oceanic Steam Navigation Company, Ltd. in 1869, in order that they might, for passenger and cargo traffic between England and America, employ similar vessels of larger size. The firm went on from triumph to triumph, breaking one record after another. The first White Star liner—the *Oceanic*—built by them in 1871, had a gross tonnage of 3918. The second *Oceanic* built twenty-eight years later, was of 17,274 gross tonnage, with an indicated horse-power of 28,000. Then followed (1904) such monster floating palaces as the *Baltic* of nearly 24,000 tons, followed by still greater marvels like the triple-screw sister ships the *Olympic* and the ill-fated *Titanic*, which was sunk

Larne, from S.W.

by collision with an iceberg in the North Atlantic on her maiden voyage. These two vessels each of 45,000 gross tonnage and 50,000 indicated horse-power, were launched in 1910 and 1911 respectively, and were followed in 1915 by the 50,000 tons *Britannic*. This vessel, which was fitted out as a hospital ship, was sunk by the enemy in the Ægean Sea.

As was only to be expected, this progress in ship-building was not only accompanied by, but was the result of, continuous and striking improvements in design. The application of the " surface condenser," the combination of low-pressure turbines with high-pressure reciprocating engines, of both these with the triple screw, the use of quadruple expansion and " balancing " are a few only of the landmarks of progress in shipbuilding. The building of these huge ships involved great extension of accommodation and equipment at Queen's Island. Thus there is a 200-ton floating crane and a huge double gantry which alone cost over a quarter of a million pounds to erect.

In addition to a large number of ships for various firms Messrs Harland & Wolff have built over fifty for the White Star Line. Prior to the war they employed in Belfast alone over 16,000 men. The name of Lord Pirrie will always be associated with this great concern. After having " gone through the shops " he was head draughtsman when the White Star liners were first designed, and was made a partner when twenty-seven years of age. On the death of Sir Edward Harland in 1895 Mr Pirrie succeeded him as Chairman of the firm, and during the war was made Controller General of Merchant Shipbuilding. To him must in large measure be attributed the striking success of the industry.

During the period of the war the resources of this great firm were put to the test and, devoting them to the common cause, they were able to turn out in the earlier years of the war first-class fighting vessels, large cruisers like the *Glorious* and monitors (*Abercrombie*, *Havelock*, *Lord Clive* and others) as well as huge mercantile armed cruisers. Later they turned their efforts to the rapid production of standard ships, as well as ships of novel type for special duties. The work of new construction during the five years 1914 to 1918 amounted, approximately, to 400,000 gross tons. Notwithstanding these titanic labours the firm carried out enormous extensions, including a new shipyard with slipways suitable for constructing vessels 700 ft. to 800 ft. long. The firm recently employed, in the Belfast works, about 21,000 men, with a weekly wage bill of about £80,000.

The second great firm referred to, that of Messrs Workman, Clark & Co., did not start their Belfast shipyard until 1879, but the period was favourable and the progress made very rapid. Indeed, in 1909, they took first place in the kingdom for the tonnage launched in that year, viz. 88,952. They have built large Allan and Orient liners installed with Parsons steam-turbine engines.

As in the case of Messrs Harland & Wolff, this firm devoted themselves almost entirely to Admiralty work during the war. They converted cruisers of an older type into monitors, and an important development was the building on to the sides of these and other vessels, projections which greatly increased the displacement but also gave protection against torpedo attack. A considerable amount of new construction work of new warships, of " Q " ships, and ships of special type was carried out.

Further important work was carried out in Londonderry by the North of Ireland Shipbuilding Co., Ltd., and at Larne by the Larne Shipbuilding Co. The developments undertaken by the former company enable them now to deal with vessels of 11,000 tons dead weight.

The value of the steam vessels built and " exported " from Ireland in 1915 was £4,721,500, and this rose to £8,056,000 in 1917.

The great linen industry has grown up during the last two centuries. Prior to 1700 only a small amount was exported, but from this date, under the stimulus of bounties amounting to from ten to fifteen per cent., the growth of the industry has, with marked fluctuations, been rapid. It is an error to suppose that in the early period of its existence it was peculiar to Ulster. Flax was hand-spun and hand-woven generally over the four provinces. To-day, indeed, a limited amount of the finer fabrics is woven on hand looms. By 1741 the value of the export of linen from Ireland reached £600,000, and by 1770 it amounted to £1,500,000. The value of linen goods exported in 1915 amounted to nearly £15,000,000, in addition to which, linen yarn to the value of £1,487,285 was exported. Though machinery had been introduced for the spinning of flax in Cork about the year 1800, it was not until about 1828 that it was introduced into Belfast. It may be noted here that at the first census in 1757 there were but 1779 houses and 8549 inhabitants of Belfast. There were then 399 looms. It is not necessary to enquire into the reasons why the north-eastern corner gradually concentrated in itself this great industry, but they are not unconnected with the Scots settlement in Ulster about 1670 and later of the Huguenots. When at last machinery was introduced, the industry began to flourish exceedingly. Flax spinning mills driven by water-power were, in and after 1805, started in various places in Ulster, and a bounty of 30s. per spindle was given to encourage the erection of mills. One of the largest of these was that of Messrs Joseph Nicholson & Son, of Bessbrook. In all, 1024 spindles were at work here. From this date until 1811 twelve spinning mills were erected in Ulster (with 6369 spindles) in the counties of Antrim, Armagh, Down, Donegal, and Tyrone, The object of the bounties was, it was stated, to render the country independent of foreign supply—the articles such as sail-cloth, etc., were suitable for use in the Navy. But these bounties were accompanied by a number of restrictions applied by a Board of Trustees of the Linen and Hempen Manufactures, a body estab-lished by Act of Parliament. It sat in Dublin, meeting weekly, and regulated the trade throughout the whole country, employing a large staff of inspectors and other officers. The bounties were finally withdrawn in 1828, and the Board ceased to be.

While the spinning of flax was carried on all over Ireland, the weaving of linen began to be concentrated in Ulster. The sale of brown linen amounted in 1815 to about two and a half million pounds annually. Lisburn produced the largest amount, Belfast came next, with Dungannon and Armagh running it closely. Ballymena, Strabane, and some thirty-three other towns also produced varying amounts. It seems probable that the position of Lisburn was due to the fact that, after the revocation of the Edict of Nantes, Louis Crommelin, who had been engaged in the linen trade in Picardy, came over to Ireland and was granted letters patent by William III. as " Overseer of the Royal Linen Manufacture of Ireland." He brought other Huguenots and settled at the small ruined village of Lisnagarvey—now Lisburn. They introduced and taught improved methods of growing and treating flax. They introduced better spinning wheels and looms, and taught how to manufacture cambrics and other fine linens. Lisburn is still the centre for the manufacture of cambrics and lawns, damasks and bordered linen. The historical association is kept alive in the words cambric which is derived from Cambrai, and diaper which, it is believed, comes from " Cloth d'Ypres." It has been suggested that the word lawn is connected with Laon.

The brown linen market was held in a hall off Donegall Street, and the White Linen Hall in the centre of Donegall Square. It was customary for the weaver who worked in his own home to bring his webs to the market and there sell them. But in the early part of last century the " middleman " was evolved, who bought yarn from the spinner in bulk and supplied the weaver with warp and weft. This so-called " manufacturer " might have some hundreds of weavers working for him, and he would collect and bring the webs to market. Thirty years or more ago as many as 20,000 webs might be offered for sale in the Saturday market. The value of these would be about £3 per web of which the weaver would receive about £1. The power-loom has now nearly accomplished—as in silk and other textile in-

dustries—the downfall of the hand-loom industry.
The supersession of the spinning-wheel was a more rapid
process. Sir William Crawford, the Chairman of the
York Street Flax Spinning Co., an undoubted authority
on the linen industry, to whose account of it we are
much indebted, estimated that in 1893 about £220,000
was paid annually for hand-loom weaving, while in 1913
the amount was only about £55,000.

The stimulus given to the flax-spinning industry
by the introduction of machinery was aided by the
introduction of wet spinning, and by improvements in
bleaching, dyeing, and other " finishing " of the woven
cloth. The application of these processes to cotton
goods led to the establishment of a large trade with
Lancashire, and there are several plants in Ulster occupied
almost exclusively with the dyeing and finishing of
cotton goods. The mild and equable climate of Ireland
permits bleaching to be carried on throughout the year,
and before the war large quantities of linen goods were
sent from Germany, Belgium, and France to be bleached
on the Ulster greens, and returned to those countries
for sale. By 1850 there were some 326,000 power
spindles in operation—to-day there are nearly a million.

A growing branch of the industry is the manufacture
of linen sewing thread, made by twisting together several
strands of linen yarn. This branch was developed
during the war, when the demand for strong linen
sewing threads for use by the army became very great,
and in peace times the threads are being exported—
particularly to Australasia.

However rapid the growth of the machine spinning
industry has been, that of the power-loom industry
has far surpassed it. Thus in 1850 there were 88 power-

looms in operation in Ireland. This number had increased to 21,779 in 1880 and 36,200 in 1908. During the war an enormous demand arose for aeroplane linen, and the product of Irish looms was found eminently suitable for the purpose.

The capital employed in the Irish linen trade at the beginning of the war was estimated at about £16,000,000.

During the last thirty years the " making-up " trade has been largely developed, and the power-driven sewing machine and the embroidery machine have greatly contributed to this development, and give employment to thousands of girls in and around Belfast. Handkerchiefs, doylies, tea-cloths, etc., are produced in large quantities. Many of these are embroidered. " Sprigging " or " flowering," as it is called, is carried on by hand mainly in the north-western counties, but has greatly declined in recent years. The decline is due to the development of the machine embroidery industry in Germany, Austria, and Switzerland. Machine embroidery has, however, been developed in Ireland, largely owing to the establishment, under the Department of Agriculture and Technical Instruction of two machine embroidery schools, one at Ballydougan in Co. Down and the other at Maghera in Co. Londonderry. The hand industry has also been fostered, both in white and coloured embroidery, through numerous classes and by special training of teachers of design and technique.

While woollen weaving is more generally carried on in the south of Ireland, there are several successful mills in the north, as in Crumlin and Caledon. Carpet weaving is carried on in Co. Donegal, where many years ago a factory for the manufacture of hand-tufted carpets was established by Mr Morton with the assistance of the Congested Districts Board. The richness and design of these carpets earned for them a high reputation.

Noteworthy among north of Ireland industries is the rope and twine manufacture of Belfast. From a small concern, intended to supply the requirements of

School of Machine Embroidery, Ballydougan, Co. Down

shipbuilding in the middle of the eighteenth century, has grown the huge industry incorporated in 1876 as the Belfast Ropework Company, Ltd., which produces ships' cables, binder twines for reaping and self-binding machines, fishing lines of all kinds, and sends its products all over the world. It employs from 3000 to 4000 workers.

Among other industries must be mentioned the

distilling of whisky and the manufacture of aerated waters. Tobacco manufacture is, too, one of Belfast's oldest industries, one firm alone turning out about 80 tons weekly.

Though the province of Ulster is noteworthy for its industrial activities it can also boast a highly developed agricultural system. The total area is over $5\frac{1}{4}$ million acres, and of this something like one-third is under crops. The proportion under corn and root crops to that under hay is also very high. The western highlands do not afford the conditions essential to successful cultivation, and in these districts the area under cultivation is relatively small. The area under corn crops is high in Down, Monaghan, Londonderry, Armagh, and Tyrone, a large quantity of wheat being grown in Down.

Ulster is, moreover, a great potato-growing province, and had over 278,000 acres under this characteristically Irish crop in 1918, over twice as much, in proportion to its area, as Munster or Leinster, and much more than Connaught. Large areas are under flax while it has 10,614 acres under fruit, that is more than the remainder of the country. It shared in the general increase of cultivation which war conditions brought about, the increase being most marked in potatoes, flax, and fruit. The cutting off of supplies of foreign flax, and the demand for aeroplane linen gave an extraordinary impetus to flax cultivation, and the acreage under this crop, which was 48,747 in 1914 rose to 89,306 in 1916 and 135,219 in 1918. It may be noted that these increases were accompanied by a decrease in the number of cattle and sheep.

The cost of food during the war gave a great impetus

to allotment gardening in the neighbourhood of large towns, and Belfast exhibited a noteworthy development in this respect. The movement in this direction began about 1907, and in the winter of 1916 the Belfast Garden Plots' Association was formed. Great success attended its efforts, and by 1919 no fewer than 4500 plots were being worked. This voluntary work was assisted by the Department and instructors made available by co-operation with the Municipal Technical Institute. Considerable attention has indeed been paid to agricultural education in Ulster. At Cookstown, in Co. Tyrone, is the Ulster Dairy School, which is managed directly by the Department. It is for the training of girls, and is open to residential pupils only. Pupils selected for instructorships complete their training at the Munster Institute, Cork. Near the town of Antrim is the Antrim Agricultural School, which conducts courses in poultry-keeping, dairying, cookery, etc., extending for nine weeks. The North-West Agricultural School at Strabane provides instruction in agriculture, veterinary hygiene, and fruit growing for young men during the winter, while there are courses for poultry-keeping, dairying, and domestic economy for young women in the spring, summer, and autumn months. Scholarships tenable here are awarded by County Committees of Agriculture.

The Congested Districts Board have, since 1891, assisted by direct action in improving the condition of the people whose holdings are not adequate to support them and their families. Since 1822 such families had suffered hunger whenever their potato crops were blighted or otherwise diseased, and this was by no means rare, especially in Donegal and other western areas. Successful efforts were made to improve the breeds of live-stock and poultry, and large sums were spent in connection with the improvements of the breeds of horses, ponies, and asses. Small holdings were enlarged and improved, and efforts directed to the encouragement of home industry.

The work of voluntary organisations, notably the

The Pork Market, Monaghan

Irish Agricultural Organisation Society, has accomplished great results. Under this organisation a very large number of Co-operative Creameries and of Agricultural Credit Societies have been established in the province, and small farmers have been induced to co-operate in various ways to their great mutual advantage.

Both the sea and the inland fisheries of Ulster constitute a valuable industry, though it suffers considerable

fluctuation from year to year. Perhaps the most noteworthy of the sea fisheries is the summer herring fishery,
of which Ardglass and Kilkeel on the Co. Down coast
are the most important centres. Very great improve-
ment has been effected in the last year or two in the
harbour accommodation at the latter place. Herring

Bann Falls, Coleraine

of the value of over £46,000 was landed at these two
fishing villages in the summer of 1917. Ardglass has
also got a fair winter herring fishery. Burtonport and
Killybegs (Co. Donegal) are the most important centres
for herring on this part of the coast. From eighty to
ninety years ago these places were the centre of a great
herring fishery, then the herrings vanished. The industry
has, however, again revived during the last quarter of
a century, and Burtonport has an important winter

fishery. Much seaweed is gathered by the fishermen on the Donegal coast. This is used on the land for manurial purposes, but much is burned to make " kelp," a valuable source of potash, for the extraction of which it is exported. Some 640 tons were exported from Donegal in 1917.

The inland fisheries are also of considerable value. The Bann and Lough Neagh fisheries are noteworthy for their yield of salmon and eel, while pollen and perch are captured in large numbers. Toomebridge, between Lough Neagh and Lough Beg in Co. Antrim has a very important eel fishery. Many of the smaller rivers provide excellent rod fishing.

DISTINGUISHED ULSTERMEN

DID space permit it would not have been difficult to extend the following list of distinguished Ulstermen. Ulster can recall with pride many great names of the past—saints, poets, and native chieftains—and can boast such names as Lord Kelvin, one of the greatest men of science of recent times ; James Macartney, F.R.S. (1770-1843), the anatomist, and the late Professor John M'Clelland, F.R.S., the eminent physicist. It has always been rich in divines : Hugh MacCaghwell (Mac Aingil), the schoolman (1571-1626) ; William King (1650-1729), the great Archbishop of Dublin, may be mentioned, and among a great number of Presbyterian divines, John Cooke and Hugh Hanna are gratefully remembered. Of men of letters Ulster can claim Henry Brooke (1706-83), the author of the *Fool of Quality*; William Drennan (1754-1820), poet and United Irishman; John Kells Ingram (1823-1907), poet, scholar, and economist; Sir Charles Gavan Duffy (1816-1903), poet and statesman; and W. B. Maxwell (1792-1850), the novelist and military historian. George Canning (1770-1827), though born in London, was of Ulster origin. The late Sir Robert Hart, the great Chinese administrator, was a Portadown man.

For notices of St Columba, Hugh O'Neill, Earl of Tyrone, and Lord Kelvin, see *Ireland* volume.

ADAMNAN, Saint (625-704), was born in south-west Donegal. He entered the monastery of Iona as a monk under Segene, and in 679 was elected abbot, and head of the Columban institutions in Ireland. One of his pupils was Aldfrid, afterwards king of Northumbria, and his intimate friend. Adamnan revisited Ireland on several occasions, in 697 at the great Synod of Tara carrying his famous enactment, known as the " Lex Adamnani," or " Cáin Adamnáin," which exempted women from battles and hostings. A strong advocate of the Roman observance of Easter, he finally succeeded in causing it to be adopted in Ireland. He lives by his *Life of Columba*, one of the most famous in hagiological literature, and, according to Montalembert, also one of the most authentic monuments of Christian history. His *De Locis Sanctis* taken down from a Frankish bishop, Arculfus, whom he entertained when shipwrecked, is one of the earliest descriptions of the Holy Land.

ALLINGHAM, William (1824-89) the poet, was born at Ballyshannon, where his father was manager of the local bank. He entered the Customs service, and spent most of his life in England. On his retirement in 1870 he became sub-editor, and afterwards editor, of *Fraser's Magazine*. He was the intimate friend of Rossetti and other members of the Pre-Raphaelite Brotherhood. A prolific writer, his exquisite lyrical talent is best seen in the collected volume *Day and Night Songs*. His ballad *The Winding Banks of Erne*, or *The Emigrant's Adieu to Ballyshannon* is perhaps the most popular of all his poems.

BUNTING, Edward (1773-1843), devoted his life to the collecting and preservation of the national music of Ireland. He was born at Armagh. His first *Collection* (1796) inspired Thomas Moore to write his *Irish Melodies*. The third *Collection* (1840) contains a valuable dissertation on ancient Irish musical instruments.

CARLETON, William (1794-1869), the novelist, was born at Prillisk, Co. Tyrone, his father being a small farmer. His early life is related in his unfinished *Autobiography*, a work entitled to rank with the great masterpieces of the kind. No one has ever succeeded in portraying the Irish peasant so faithfully without caricature or exaggeration. He wrote many novels, but *Traits and Stories of the Irish Peasantry* is his best known work. He was also a poet of merit, his *Sir Turlough, or the Churchyard Bride*, being, according to Sir Theodore Martin, the most successful legendary ballad of modern times.

COLGAN, John (d. 1658), the hagiologist, was born near the village of Carn, in Donegal. He entered the Franciscan Order and was for a time Professor of Theology at the Irish College, Louvain. With Hugh WARD (d. 1635), also a Donegal man, and his Superior, he projected a great work on the ecclesiastical history and antiquities of Ireland, the *Acta Sanctorum Hiberniæ*. Ward unhappily did not live to see it published, and to

Colgan it fell to bring out the first volume. Patrick
FLEMING, and Michael O'CLERY [*q.v.*], co-operated in
this great undertaking, which, though never completed,
remains an enduring monument of vast learning and
research, one of the glories of the Irish Church. Only
two volumes appeared, the first (1645) containing the
Saints of the first quarter, the second, entitled *Trias
Thaumaturga* (1647) containing the collected lives of
Patrick, Columba, and Brigit. Colgan also published a
Tractatus on *Duns Scotus* (1655), in which he sought to
prove the Irish origin of the subtle doctor.

COMGALL of Bangor (c. 516-601), a saint of the First
Order, was a native of Magheramorne, Co. Antrim. He
founded the great monastic school of Bangor in Co.
Down, where he is said to have had as many as 3000
students under him at one time. His most distinguished
pupil was Columbanus, who carried the Rule of Bangor,
still extant, to the Appenines. The *Antiphonary of
Bangor* (seventh century), one of the oldest monuments
of Western liturgy, contains a hymn in honour of St
Comgall.

DUFFERIN and AVA, Frederick Temple Blackwood,
first Marquis (1826-1902), diplomatist, son of Lord
Dufferin, of Clandeboye, Co. Down, was born at Florence,
Italy. He filled the highest diplomatic posts in the
British empire, having been Governor-General of Canada
(1872-8), Viceroy of India (1884-8), and Ambassador at
Petrograd (1879-81), Constantinople (1881-2), Rome
(1888-91), and Paris (1891-6) He was created an earl
in 1871 for his services in connection with the Turco-
Egyptian question, and a marquis in 1888 on the annexa-
tion of Upper Burma. He was a polished and refined
orator, and his *Letters from High Latitudes* (1860),

display his inherited literary gifts. His mother, a grand-daughter of Sheridan, was the author of the touching *Lament of the Irish Emigrant*, and many other beautiful ballads.

FARQUHAR, George (1678-1707), the most brilliant of

The First Marquis of Dufferin and Ava

the comic dramatists of the Restoration, was born at Londonderry, and educated at Trinity College, Dublin. His finest plays are *The Recruiting Officer* and *The Beaux' Stratagem*. He was for a time in the Army, and excels in the representation of military characters.

FERGUSON, Sir Samuel (1810-86), poet and antiquary,

born at Belfast, came of a Scottish family long settled in the North of Ireland. After a successful career at the bar, he became Deputy-Keeper of the Records. Though a distinguished antiquary (he was President of the Royal Irish Academy), he lives as one of the greatest of Irish poets. In no other is the old Gaelic spirit and the supreme art of a great poet combined in such a degree as in Ferguson. His longer poems *Congal, Conary,* and *Deirdre,* founded on old Irish sagas, represent him at his best. *Conary* has been described as "the noblest English poem ever written by an Irishman." His best known prose works are the *Hibernian Nights' Entertainments,* and the amusing dialogue *Father Tom and the Pope.*

FINNIAN of Moville (d. 579), the patron saint of Ulster, was of the royal house of the Dál Fiatach. He founded the celebrated school at Mag Bile (Moville), near Strangford Lough, where Columba was one of his pupils. A great collector of manuscripts, and student of the scriptures, he brought home from Rome about 540 a copy of the Gospels, said, on good evidence, to have been the first copy of Jerome's translation introduced into Ireland, and the exemplar of the Book of Durrow. The copy made from it surreptitiously by Columba was the cause of the historic judgment : " To every cow her calf, and to every book its transcript."

HUTCHESON, Francis (1694-1747), the philosopher, was born in Down, at Drumalig. He studied at Glasgow University, where he was for many years Professor of Moral Philosophy. He is regarded as the founder of the Scottish school of Metaphysics, and also of modern æsthetic criticism, and he is said to have been the precursor of the Utilitarian school, being the first to use the

phrase " the greatest happiness of the greatest number."
His chief works are *An Inquiry into the Original of our
Ideas of Beauty and Virtue* (1725), and *A System of Moral
Philosophy* (1755).

Sir Henry Lawrence

LAWRENCE, Sir Henry (1806-57), and his brother
John, Lord LAWRENCE (1811-79), though both born out
of Ireland were of a county Derry family, their father,

Colonel Lawrence, being a native of Coleraine. Both brothers were educated at Derry. They both played a notable part in the administration of India, particularly in the settlement of the Punjaub. Sir Henry Lawrence, who was a distinguished soldier, was mortally wounded during the siege of Lucknow. His brother, who has been called " the saviour of India," ultimately became Governor-General of India, and was created a peer.

MAC CULLAGH, James (1809-47), the mathematician, was born at Landahussy, Co. Tyrone, and educated at Trinity College, Dublin. His investigations into the laws governing the motion of light brought him fame and honours. It is to his liberality and public spirit that Dublin owes the beautiful and priceless Cross of Cong, which he presented to the Museum of the Royal Irish Academy.

MITCHEL, John (1815-75), patriot and man of letters, was born at Camnish, Co. Londonderry, the son of a Unitarian minister. He was for a time editor of *The Nation*, and in 1848 started *The United Irishman* newspaper. His writings have had a powerful influence on national thought to the present day. His brilliant style and unrivalled wit is best seen in his *Jail Journal* (1856), and *The Last Conquest of Ireland (Perhaps)* (1860). He also wrote a *History of Ireland from the Treaty of Limerick* (1869).

O'CLERY, Michael (1575-1643), the chief of the Four Masters, one of the greatest names in Irish literature, was born at Kilbarron, near Ballyshannon, and died at Louvain, a lay brother in the Franciscan Order. Being a noted Irish scholar, he was sent to Ireland by Hugh Ward to collect materials for his *Acta Sanctorum*. In

this undertaking O'Clery laboured fifteen years, and
compiled from ancient sources in the Convent of Donegal

John Mitchel

his greatest work, the *Annals of the Kingdom of Ireland*,
commonly called *Annals of the Four Masters* : his colla-
borators being Conaire O'Clery, his brother ; Cucogry

or Peregrine O'Clery, his cousin, the author of a *Life of Red Hugh O'Donnell*; and Fearfeasa O'Mulconry. He also compiled the *Book of Conquests* (Leabhar Gabhála), the *Martyrologium* or *Calendar of Irish Saints*, and several genealogical works. The only work published in his lifetime was his precious *Glossary* (Foclóir nó Sanasan Nua), Louvain, 1643. Two centuries elapsed before his other great works, all left ready for press, with the necessary approbations, were published and translated.

O'HUSSEY, Eochaidh (fl. 1600), in Irish, Ó hEoghusa, the greatest Irish poet of his time, was chief bard to the Maguires, lords of Fermanagh. His *Ode to Hugh Maguire* is widely known through Mangan's rendering, " Where is my Chief, my Master, this bleak night, Mavrone ? "

O'NEILL, Owen Roe (c. 1582-1649), Irish patriot and general, was son of Art and nephew of Hugh O'Neill [*q.v.* IRELAND volume], whom he probably met on the Continent, on the flight of the Earls (1607). He was educated at the Irish College, Louvain, and entered the Spanish service. He greatly distinguished himself by his defence of Arras (1640) against a greatly superior French force, being allowed to march out with full military honours on capitulating. In 1642 he returned to Ireland as commander of the Ulster forces in the Revolutionary War. He inflicted a sanguinary defeat on the Scottish army under Monro at Benburb in 1646, the sole victory gained by the Irish in this war. He was by far the ablest of native Irish generals.

SLOANE, Sir Hans (1660-1753), the eminent physician and naturalist, was born at Killyleagh, Co. Down. His most important work was *A Voyage to the Islands of*

u M

Madeira . . . and Jamaica, with the natural history of the last (1707-25). In 1727 he succeeded Sir Isaac Newton as President of the Royal Society. His magnificent collections of natural history, antiquities, books, manuscripts, coins, etc. bequeathed to the nation, formed the nucleus of what is now the British Museum.

THOMPSON, William (1805-52), the naturalist, was born at Belfast. His *Natural History of Ireland* (1849-51), was completed after his death by his friend, Robert Patterson, F.R.S. (1802-72), also a Belfast man and a distinguished zoologist.

WALKER, George (1618-90), the heroic defender of Londonderry in the memorable siege of 1688, was born in Co. Tyrone. Though an old man at the outbreak of the Revolution, he raised a regiment at his own expense. He published his *True Account of the Siege* in 1689, and fell in the following year at the Battle of the Boyne. He had just been designated Bishop of Derry by William III.

WARD, Owen, in Irish Eoghan Ruadh MAC AN BHAIRD (d. 1609), was chief bard of the O'Donnells, Earls of Tirconnell. His fine *Lament for the Princes of Tyrone and Tirconnell* who died in exile has been immortalised by Mangan : " O woman of the Piercing Wail, Who mournest o'er yon mound of clay."

WHITE, Sir George Stuart (1835-1912), Field-Marshal, was born at Rock Castle, Portstewart, Co. Antrim. He took part in many campaigns, winning the V.C. in the Afghan War of 1879. He was in command of the forces in Burma, 1886-9, and Commander-in-Chief in India, 1893-8 ; he succeeded Lord Roberts. His heroic defence of Ladysmith (1899-1900) is one of the most memorable in military history.

INDEX

u M*

Gowna, Lough, 6, 16, 42
Granite, 7, 12, 40, 46, 52, 58, 67,
    red, 76
    setts, 75
Great Church, Devenish, 128
Greenisland, 22
Grey Abbey, 123
Griánán Ailigh, 117
Gypsum, 46, 54, 71

Hæmatite, 68
Hanna, Hugh, 168
Harland, Edward James, 154
Harland & Wolff, 151
Hart, Sir Robert, 169
High Crosses, 122
Hilltown, 12
Horn Head, 30, 92
Huguenot settlers, 159, 160
Hutchison, Francis, 173

Inch Abbey, 125
    Island, 66
Ingram, John Kells, 169
Inishowen, 3, 9, 25, 30, 66
Inishtrahull, 30
Irish Agricultural Organisation
    Society, 166
Irish Rat, 89
Irish Speakers, 5
Iron ore, 59, 68
Irvinestown, 73
Island Magee, 27

Jordan's Castle, Ardglass, 137

Keady, 71
Kelp burning, 168
Kelvin, Lord, 168
Kemper Stone Dolmen, 107
Kettle holes, 65
Kilbarron Castle, 137
Kilcloony dolmen, 107
Kilcrea, 71
Kilkeel, 12, 167
    river, 12

Kilmore Cathedral, 134
Kilrea, 36
Killybegs, 25, 31, 34, 167
Kinale, Lough, 6
Kingscourt, 54, 76
King William, 168
Kirkistone Castle, 138
Knockagh, the, 22
Knocklay, 10
Knockmany tumulus, 109
Knockmore precipice, 14

Lagan, the, 2, 18, 22, 25, 38,
    40, 54, 64, 152
Lakes, 15, 40, 42, 76, 90
Landslides, 55
Larne, 10, 22, 23, 27, 39, 72, 103
    aluminium works, 70
    "celts," 104
    Lough, 27, 39
    shipyards, 151
Lava, 57, 58
Lawrence, Sir Henry, 174
    Lord John, 174
Lead ore, 71
Legananny dolmen, 107
Letterkenny, 34
Lifford, 34
Limavady, 36
Lime-burning, 72
Limestone, 7, 14, 31, 42, 46,
    53, 59, 72
Limonite, 69
Linen industry, 10, 15, 39, 40,
    41, 151, 158
Lisburn, 10, 18, 39, 73, 159
    cathedral, 134
    Huguenot settlement, 160
Lisnacroghera crannog, 101,
    120
Lisnagarvey, Huguenot settle-
    ment, 160
Londonderry, 18, 21, 22, 23, 29,
    34, 66, 140, 142
    cathedral, 132
    county, 31, 34, 140
    Foyle College, 149

For EU product safety concerns, contact us at Calle de José Abascal, 56–1°, 28003 Madrid, Spain or eugpsr@cambridge.org.

www.ingramcontent.com/pod-product-compliance
Ingram Content Group UK Ltd.
Pitfield, Milton Keynes, MK11 3LW, UK
UKHW020308140625
459647UK00014B/1791